PROPHECY NOW

Planet Out of Balance

Book Titles by Betsey Lewis

Lizzie Extraterrestrials Worldwide
Signals from Heaven
Prophecy 2022
Stargates
Extraterrestrial Encounters of The Extraordinary Kind
Star Beings
Déjà vu
Ancient Serpent Gods
Mystic Revelations of Seven
Mystic Revelations of Thirteen
Baffled by Their Brilliance
Earth Energy: Return to Ancient Wisdom
Communicating with the Other Side

More books by Betsey on Amazon

Spiritual Books for Children
Alexander Phoenix
The Story of Rainbow Eyes
A Worm Named Sherm

PROPHECY NOW

Planet Out of Balance

Betsey Lewis

Prophecy Now: Planet out of Balance

Copyright © 2022 Betsey Lewis

ISBN: 979-8842756995

Cover design by Betsey Lewis (4)

TABLE OF CONTENTS

Prophecy Now

For the Family of Light

"We will declare frankly that nothing is clear in this world. Only fools and charlatans know and understand everything." —Anton Chekhov, Russian playwright (1890-1904)

CHAPTER ONE

Planet Out of Balance

Earth and humanity are out of balance. There's a great imbalance in our world, both in the physical and spiritual world. Humans have lost their way and we have forgotten how to be grateful for their lives and having the opportunity to be here at this monumental time. We are experiencing a time of profound unprecedented change. Change is oftentimes unpredictable and how you handle chaos in this timeline is a test of your ability to evolve and change—change creates new experiences, and this is how we learn. But sometimes we need to be shaken to the very core of our souls to change.

Your challenge at this time is to gain your innate freedom, and this does not involve fighting the government, the military, your fellow human, or any other forces that appear to trap you in 3-D.

It's time to buckle up for the ride of your life. Remember you didn't sign up for easy. As the Family of Light, you go into systems to create change and balance.

Many of you have been a bit naïve, and too willing to play their game of control, listening to those in authority and doing what you are told like a robot instead of using critical thinking, intuition, and common sense. People are not encouraged to think for themselves. Mass programming is in effect all over the world and you are taught what to think. This type of misuse of energy can only go so far before humans become disconnected and compartmentalized fragments without a connection to the whole. When the system becomes too fragmented, eventually it collapses on itself. Because most of you have been fed a series of false beliefs for eons, each person on Earth has become compartmentalized in what he or she believes and unable to use real thinking.

Already the old paradigm is breaking down and light is changing life on Earth. People are beginning to awaken and sometimes that awakening can be uncomfortable. The time has arrived to stop letting the controllers that live in the dark from controlling us.

The way to disconnect from mind control is to wean yourself from television, radio, and cell phones that send frequencies to control you. As events speed up, it will be imperative for each of you to slow down with nature. Nature has much to teach us—it's the living library. Listen to the birds, a crackling fire, and the wind through the trees. Get outdoors more and stop being couch potatoes. Expand your awareness and listen to your inner voice, your higher consciousness, because as things accelerate you will need to be alert and aware of what is happening.

As our system collapses, and it will, because it is so out of balance, familiar comforts will disappear rapidly—food shortages, oil and gas shorts, and many other creature comforts and you will need to think on all cylinders. You can't be stoned on marijuana, drinking to excess, or using other drugs. You need a clear mind.

A force of psychic spiritual energy will explode, creating rapid changes on a planetary scale. Do you think that all the UFO sightings are drones like the Pentagon and military want you to believe? They are here to assist and awaken humanity to their presence.

Whoever is placed in positions of authority—governments, religious leaders, educational systems, kings, priests, popes, politicians, or presidents—their power will be questioned. This is a time when power will return to the people.

Think about the uniqueness of Earth and why it's been called the "Goldilock's planet." Remember the children's story, *Goldilocks and the Three Bears*? In the story, a little girl named Goldilocks liked everything perfect. Her porridge couldn't be too hot or too cold. And her bed couldn't be too hard or too soft. On Earth, the atmosphere and everything are perfect for life to thrive.

Unfortunately, most of us take Earth and our lives on this planet for granted. Earth is a mystery and there are an infinite number of mysteries on our planet.

Our knowledge of Earth and the Universe is comparable to a single grain of sand in the ocean. In my seventy-two years of life, I have learned a lot about human nature, some good, and other things that aren't so good. Perhaps my greatest disappointment would be the way we treat each other with prejudices, racism, hate for one another, wars, and the lack of compassion and love for our fellow humans, Earth's creatures, and our fragile environment.

You'd think that after 300,000 years (according to anthropologists) modern humans (Homo Erectus) would have evolved into spiritual beings with a reverence for all life. But we haven't. Wars are raging, people are enslaved, people are killed for the color of their skin, their religious beliefs, their sexual preference, their politics, and on and on. I believe that somewhere in the Universe or multiverses there are kind and peaceful beings who honor each other and the life on their planet. If I was a visiting alien to Earth, I'd never stop to learn about humans. It's just too crazy— *en mass* the negative consciousness of humanity permeates into the Cosmos, and spiritual aliens feel it.

Earth is beautiful and continually demonstrates the harmony and interconnectedness of all things, which is a great lesson. With

All the Is or God, there is no ego, no ambition, no competition, no hatred, no fear, and no enemies. There is only light and the embrace of love.

Once a light of truth and knowledge was taught by ancient Masters who walked upon the Earth and left us teachings to live by. Much of what those masters taught us thousands of years ago while on Earth has been lost or reinterpreted. In the last one hundred years, humanity has spiraled downward in spirituality.

Until we learn that we have a mystical and symbiotic relationship with all life, our planet will continue to become more erratic from the weather, volcanic eruptions, and solar eruptions to increasing destructive earthquakes. Another hurricane could still hit Florida in 2022. Human consciousness *en mass* is powerful enough to create harmony and peace or chaos and war. We allowed the chaos on our planet by becoming powerless. Many who walk this Earth are godless and soul-less. They consider themselves above us.

The eyes are the windows to the soul, and that is true. If you look into the eyes of some of our leaders, their eyes are devoid of compassion and love.

There will come a time when you look deep into the eyes of another human, you will see your soul looking back at you, and then you will know that you have reached a higher level of consciousness. Remember when you awaken to the mind control that has been used on the planet, a great understanding will spring forth into a very great light of awareness and truth, and a new dawning in the art of thinking, birthing a renaissance of creative being. The control will stop!

As you learn about how you have been controlled and influenced, you will realize how easy it is to feed your data. Whether it is through electronic repetition or occult misuse of power through sexuality, and murders. There are many ways to fragment and compartmentalize the human brain through brainwashing. Millions of children have been sexually abused and their minds become compartmentalized from the abuse to survive.

Humans must learn that we create our world with our minds,

our daily thoughts, our words, and our actions. Where do you think all the energy goes? Thoughts form physical reality.

You have been taught that you are alone in the universe so that you will be more manageable. We've been told that our ancestors were apes, but that is far from the truth. Great civilizations existed millions of years ago, and their technology exists in megalithic stone today. Do you really believe a bunch of Egyptian slaves toiled night and day to build the Great Pyramid of Giza? There are legends and stories worldwide that stones can float in the air. When I visited the Maya temple Xunantunich in Belize in 1993, I swam across the Mopan River with a friend to explore the temple after hours. We were met by two friendly Mayan caretakers. One spoke English and told us that the Maya people could make stones fly. They had the technology of levitation. Our scientists today are just beginning to learn levitation.

In my prophecy books, I have pointed out that we are the Atlanteans returned. Thousands of years ago, the Atlanteans reached the pinnacle of science and technology, but there were great divisions among the people and a war between the spiritual and the unspiritual took place. Some were spiritually balanced and there were those consumed in greed to control the world through their advanced sciences. Sadly, we still haven't learned the lessons of balance, love, kindness, and compassion for each other.

Many of you are having visions of other worlds, astral projecting, and wondering if Earth is your true home. That feeling of not belonging started when you were a child. You may have seen the future and spirits, and recalled past lives. Millions of children are seeing these things, but don't know where to turn to discuss their paranormal experiences. Often children are told to hush up, and not say anything about their unusual experiences for fear of being punished. I was lucky that my mother believed in the supernatural and extraterrestrials, and we had many incredible conversations through the years of her experiences and mine.

When I have a vision, it happens suddenly and without any warning. One minute I am in this world, and the next I am viewing the future like a movie. I have foreseen many events from megathrust earthquakes, hurricanes, assassinations, Queen Elizabeth's death, and celebrity births to the election of President Donald Trump six months before he was elected.

In *Prophecy Now*, I cover predictions on world leaders, possible World War III, a nuclear weapon exploding in Europe, the Mid-term election in the U.S., UK's King Charles and his future, UK's Prince Harry and Meghan, Trump, Biden, Governor DeSantis, House Speaker Pelosi, mid-term elections on November 8, 2022, COVID and the vaccines, the crazy weather, Planet X, new inventions, volcanoes awakening, earthquakes, AI technology, chemtrails, spiraling inflation, gas prices, interest rates soaring, inflation, depression, shortages of heating, shortages of food and water, the possibility of nuclear war, Ukraine, Russian, China, drought, oil and diesel shortages, Moon launch, UFOs, wildfires, and where we are headed as a species on Mother Earth.

When it comes to foreseeing the future for a certain person, what I foresee at the moment was the path they considered, but that person and all of us have free will to change the course of our lives. We are not puppets on a string controlled by the Gods.

In previous prophecy books, some reviewers have berated my prophecies for including politics, but politics determine our future. Most people want to know what will happen with the current president and who will be elected in 2024. Our leaders determine our fate, but we also determine our fate by our actions and thoughts. Have you noticed since President Joe Biden was elected in 2020, things have deteriorated in America as I predicted? Gas prices have increased to the point people are taking two jobs to support their families, grocery prices are sky rocking, interest rates rising, and inflation, five million illegal migrants have flooded the United States in over two years from many countries and many are criminals, and drug cartels. Crime is out of control in major cities and it's like the old wild West where you can be shot or stabbed for no reason at all. A large percentage are terrorists from 165 countries sneaking into America. Our major cities are no longer safe for anyone as killings escalate and businesses are looted or burned.

Many of the growing population of homeless people in the

cities are either insane or drug-induced zombies. It is sad for them, us, and the planet, because they are lowering the vibration rate of Mother Earth. There is also the problem of dark possession by entities that want to control humans. When a human drinks or does drugs in excess, they invite dark entities into their bodies. *The Exorcist,* written by my step-uncle William Peter Blatty, was based in part on a true story of possession.

Some have their eyes wide shut to what is happening in the world. They refuse to hear anything but their own words of ignorance. Some are doubters who prefer to don rose-colored glasses and never listen with an open mind. But one day, they will have an epiphany and see the truth of their reality. Some know the truth, who sense what is taking place to our planet and our freedom. In these critical times, listen to and heed your heart and the call out to ancient wisdom and your angels.

If any of you can say, you are better off now than when Trump was President from 2016 to 2020, even with COVID hit, you are living in an alternate reality. I will tell you what is happening and where we are headed on the world stages and what I foresee for Europe and the rest of the world in 2023.

Your intense response to my predictions and blog has been overwhelming. There is a wonderful mass awareness dawning with the spirits of humans worldwide. Take heart that what you do to help the world will be carried into the next decade. When times are really tough, heroes appear, and kindness becomes contagious.

What happens in one tiny place in the world affects all of us. People sense the coming Great Unifying Event. We have felt the stirrings in our souls, retaining ancient memories of Atlantis and what happened to this great ancient continent that was destroyed due to ignorance, power, and greed. Those of you who have heard the call, are ready for this important time to join forces for the prime purpose of nourishing the Sacred Tree of Life.

The Family of Light is here at this moment to electrify the whole planet with new energy. One day in the far future, everyone will know that they are the Family of Light. You are going to be asked about your priorities—is your life and the life of your family and friends more important than your material possessions? Floods, hurricanes, wildfires, and other natural disasters will test you, and some of you will perish. Many of the lessons of day-to-day life will challenge us, and our relationships, but it's all about finding the value in living. What do morals and integrity mean to you? Do you go out of your way to help a person in need as our world goes belly-up in these most outrageous times?

All I can tell you is buckle up and keep your faith in God. Tough times ahead for all no matter where you live. May God guide you, your families, and your friends. I pray that every soul weathers the coming storms ahead. Let's all become the Butterfly in the Hurricane flapping our spiritual wings to create a new reality

Two things are infinite: The universe and human stupidity; and I'm not sure about the universe. —Albert Einstein

CHAPTER TWO

Covid Frequency Change

In 2019, a Prime Event happened that changed the world and the Earth's future. We jumped into a parallel world when COVID-19 was unleashed on the world. It was planned that way to control and alter human DNA for control. On September 11, 2001, another Prime Event took place in the twenty-first century that altered our future by taking more of our freedom away. These events shocked the world and affected the very core of our souls.

World programmers know that creating a prime event such as September 11, 2001, and the COVID-19 pandemic would create a ripple in the time continuum and alter future events. For example— time is like a speeding train headed down the tracks to the future. But the train conductor can switch the direction of the rails or an object on the tracks can stop it at any time. This is called free will. The events of 9/11 were used to see how programmable humans can be. Suddenly, our family and friends were barred from greeting us as they stepped off their flight. More than a fifth of the U.S. population is too young to remember what air travel was like before Sept. 11, 2001. Our family and friends loved to greet us or bid us farewell at the gate. Travelers were never required to take off their shoes and belts or remove liquids from carry-on luggage before going through checkpoints, let alone long security lines that included x-ray machines to detect weapons. The TSA (Transportation Security Administration) an agency of the United States Department of Homeland Security was given the authority over the security of transportation systems within and connecting to the United States. They treated us like herded cattle.

Prime Events don't need to be horrible or evil events, they can be positive. The Harmonic Convergence on August 16-17, 1987, was a positive Prime Event, organized by Dr. Jose Argüelles without the aid of the internet before it was invented. This was the world's first synchronized global peace meditation. The event coincided with an exceptional alignment of the planets in the Solar System, and two years later the Berlin Wall fell. This was a pivotal event in world history that marked the falling of the Iron Curtain and one of the series of events that started the fall of communism in Eastern and Central Europe, preceded by the Solidarity Movement in Poland.

The Harmonic Convergence was an orchestrated event impulsed from the future. It was sent from the future into the past and then reorganized into the present to create a hole through which the secondary and tertiary nets could be built and find a link to the planet.

What if consciousness controls time and created physical matter? Some authors suggest that consciousness creates timelines, and we are responsible for the events happening in our world with mass consciousness. An excellent example of mass consciousness was detected on September 11, 2001, when two National Oceanic and Atmospheric Administrations (NOAA) space weather satellites known as GOES-8 and GOES-10 that monitor the Earth's geomagnetic field picked up a huge spike as the planes hit the

World Trade Towers. It is theorized the spike recorded stress waves caused by mass human emotions on the Earth's geomagnetic field. When GOES-8 was orbiting around the equator that day at 22,000 miles above the Earth, it detected the first surge that topped out at nearly 50 units (nanoteslas) higher than any reading previously recorded. A nanotesla is a unit of measurement of a magnetic field, equal to one billionth of a tesla. The time was 9 a.m. Eastern standard time, 15 minutes after the first plane hit the World Trade Center and 15 minutes before the second impact.

The spike in the geomagnetic field was not a coincidence. Everything on this planet is connected in ways we can't imagine. We are connected to everything—the Earth, the rocks, the wind, the weather, the plants, the animals, the sun, the moon, and the oceans. The Lakota Sioux says, Mitakuye Oyasin, which means we are all related or all are related—this is what the ancient and indigenous people have known for eons.

Timelines and tributaries that run this fabric of time are linked to primary events. Without primary events, an event could not hook into a timeline and change it. Examples of prime events are the splitting of the atom. What if God's consciousness-controlled time and created physical matter? Some authors suggest that consciousness creates timelines, and we are responsible for the events happening in our world with mass consciousness.

So, without primary events, a timed event could not hook into a timeline and change it. Another example of a prime event was the splitting of the atom—the atomic bomb.

When COVID hit and spread with lightning speed around the planet, our leaders became tyrants and issued mandates for us to sequester ourselves and our children, shut down restaurants, and stay away from other humans. At first, we were told not to wear face masks by Dr. Fauci, and then *this poor excuse* for a doctor decided we had to wear them everywhere. A few months later, Dr. Fauci told us to wear two masks to save ourselves from the deadly virus.

Then came the untested vaccines, and the world became human guinea pigs for Big Pharma, but their intentions were not for the good of humanity but to get richer from human suffering. It was another way to control us. We weren't allowed to voice our opinions or mention anything about horrible side effects and deaths caused by the COVID vaccines on social media — Facebook, Twitter, and YouTube. They censored or banned us.

Why would anyone take an experimental drug? Fear! We were told that without the COVID vaccines, we would die. We were told it prevented the disease and the spread, but that was a lie. We were told it was a disease of the unvaccinated when in truth, those who were getting vaccinated were spreading the disease. The vaccines were never meant to stop the spread of the disease, but to help people with their natural immunity fight it. In many cases, it did not help but caused horrible side effects — paralysis in the face (singer Justin Bieber had this), myocarditis (inflammation of the heart muscle) and pericarditis (inflammation of the lining outside the heart), brain fog, strokes, and some who never had any health issues tragically dropped dead within days of the COVID-19 vaccine. The news media, the CDC, Dr. Fauci, and politicians covered up the truth about the vaccines.

A large number of adults had natural immunity and didn't need vaccines and children had immunity to the virus. However, a new RSV flu is putting hundreds of children in hospitals across the U.S.

Fear is the perfect way to control the masses. It's been used for ages, and our controllers are well-versed in the art of fear. These beings don't care about the masses; they only care about greed, power, and control. They feed on your fears.

Vaccines have done wonders for preventing many diseases. That is a fact. But with the COVID-19 vaccine, it was rushed into production and never tested. People were frightened and felt that was their only alternative to survive the virulent virus. Scenes of people dying alone in hospitals were carried on major news stations. That was a powerful persuader.

The controllers pushed COVID vaccines and boosters on the world even though horrible side effects and deaths were taking place, but the pharmaceutical companies, our political leaders, and mainstream news, CBS, MSNBC, ABC, and CNN, decided to hide the deaths caused by the many vaccines and boosters. And made these people just as culpable as the Chinese releasing the virus from the Wuhan laboratory throughout the world. And the social media censored anyone posting what they claimed was "disinformation" about the COVID vaccines.

This was one of the greatest attempts at genocide against humanity. It was pure evil! Nearly 7 million souls perished from COVID in two years.

To this day, I know that COVID-19 wasn't an accident. It was another way to create a negative long-lasting Prime Event on the world. We shifted into another frequency. Sadly, I wish more people would have listened to my warnings in my prophecy books and on my website blog about the vaccine side effects, but humans are stubborn beings who buy into the propaganda. We keep hearing about the "science" and people trust the government no matter what they say. I was blessed to have spirit guides who warned me against the vaccines.

When people are so overcome with fear, they don't think straight or listen to their intuition/sixth sense. They become easily swayed by false information. That's what happened. I watched as family members took the vaccine and caught COVID, and I watched how a friend and one family member who had some health issues before COVID, succumbed shortly after receiving the vaccine.

COVID will never disappear. The virus is here to stay but has mutated greatly and become the bad flu, but people still die from the flu viruses. Our world is full of sick people from our environment, water, over-processed food, sugar, and GMO corn products. The controllers want us lazy, obese humans, and that makes us more vulnerable to disease. So far, the grim consensus is they are succeeding until we awaken to what they are doing to us.

Thousands and thousands of people died in hospitals around the world, isolated from family and friends in their last hours of life. They were subject to an alien world with hospital staff wearing masks and hazmat suits. They were frightened. Others believed they couldn't die from COVID, and they and countless others are now trapped in hospitals existing on the Other Side in the bardos in-between world because they can't accept their death. Spirit guides and angels try to coax them from their self-created bardos, but they refuse to listen. From all the suffering those souls endured in their last hours of life, alone, scared, and wearing an oxygen mask, many of them are trapped on the earthly plane. I ask the next time you visit a hospital or are admitted to one, that you say a prayer for the trapped souls and tell them to go to the Light, that their spirit family, friends, and spirit guides await them on the Other Side with an outpouring of love.

There are documented cases of haunted hospitals, but so far no one has reported massive hauntings in present-day hospitals from COVID deaths. Not yet anyway. I'd love to hear from any of you who have witnessed a ghost in one of your local hospitals.

As I predicted in previous prophecy books since 2021, COVID would mutate and become like the flu. And as we all know the flu does kill people, especially those who are immune compromised by cancer, have other health issues, and the elderly. COVID will always be with us, but not like it was in the beginning. In late 2019, I had a vision of a virus like the Spanish Flu that would emerge in the coming months, but I could fathom such a virus infecting millions and killing over six million humans globally in the twenty-first century. I let my conscious mind alter my vision.

COVID was poorly handled in the United States, Canada, Australia, China, and other places. People were treated like lepers, their businesses were forced to close, and people lost their jobs if they did not conform to the mask and vaccine mandates. People poured their hearts out to me about how they had to get the vaccines or lose their jobs. Firing Federal workers because they won't take the vaccines is illegal, but it's still happening. Federal workers were fired, airplane pilots walked off their jobs or were fired as well as those in the military, firefighters, police, nurses, and doctors. There was no such thing as a religious exemption. To me, that is Draconian tyranny (Nazi laws excessively harsh and severe) against humanity. People should have been given a choice of what to put into their bodies, especially with an experimental drug being pushed worldwide by the major pharmaceutical companies and those who had stock in them.

Dr. Fauci was the poster boy of health misinformation. He claimed Ivermectin and monoclonal therapy didn't work, and people needed the vaccines, but reports began to show people dying, and children experiencing myocarditis and pericarditis problems after COVID-19 vaccines. Pilots were dying also while in flight, and this was covered up by the news media. I know for a fact a doctor friend who prescribed Ivermectin to a man dying from COVID and within days he improved and was finally able to go home a few days later despite being on his deathbed days before. I read more about these incredible stories of Ivermectin curing people of COVID, but Big Pharma didn't like us taking something simple that had the potential to help people. Ivermectin lies were spread across the internet and on television by the woke media and politicians and monoclonal therapy was banned. I had a friend and her husband in the Denver Hospital, and they were not doing well. Their doctor refused to prescribe Ivermectin. Thankfully after a month of hospitalization, they were able to go home.

Google, Facebook, Twitter, and all the other social media platforms censored anything written against the COVID vaccines. In fact, today if you search for certain information, it has been expunged from the internet by draconian corporations. They don't want you to know the truth about their dark agenda. Even today if you search for 9-11 and the conspiracy theories on how building seven collapsed without being hit by a plane, you will find videos that debunk the United States' involvement, and how the building was brought down by terrorists and not implosions. Even videos suggesting why Building Seven collapsed without a terrorist plane hitting it has been removed from YouTube.

The Family of Dark has reached total control of our world and total control over freedom of speech. This is what happened in Nazi Germany during World War II, and we are repeating this horrific history. The mainstream media repeats certain words over and over to mind control you into their woke ideologies. If Republicans reveal something, they tell you the opposite. It's all MAGA lies. You think that certain television shows protect you from certain frequencies broadcast to you. Many frequencies are hidden in documentaries, commercials, and television shows. It's all about control.

Have you noticed how long commercials have become lately? They last five minutes or more. On the Fox *9-1-1* television drama, one night the total commercials lasted 30 minutes in the one-hour show. We are bombarded by pharmaceutical ads. How many of you watch a commercial and decide to call your doctor about a certain drug that promises a cure for something, despite all the side effects including death?

In this age of instant information, you are steered away from the natural sources of gathering knowledge for yourself. You have been convinced that television is a great source of information. It's one of the greatest inventions in history. However, the media is owned and controlled by those who wish to keep you entertained and in the dark. They peddle alternate realities and fantasies. What is happening is that television slows down your evolutionary process and limits you, especially young impressionable children, especially now with all the woke, racial, and sexual teachings.

You are being kept in a narrow frequency to watch violence, protests, anger, hate, and racism. The motto for newscasters is "if it bleeds, it leads." Learn how to observe how you feel when you watch television. Chaos and fear are being rapidly promoted all over the planet through television and cell phones. You are being hypnotized by television at this very moment. It is better that you wean yourself off these controlling devices as soon as possible so you can tap into your sixth sense again, your higher self, and your spirit guides. You are suppressing your imagination and do not use one of the greatest gifts you possess — free will.

In the future, centuries from now, it will be understood that in the latter part of the twentieth century and the twenty-first century that people and children were induced into a hypnotic state for control. Remember imagination and creativity are what forms the reality in which you live. If you don't think for yourself, you can't create reality. Some of you might think that there are some good programs on television and some educational shows, but have you considered what is being beamed over or under the so-called "good programs." Frequency waves are transmitted through your television set even when you do not have it on. Unplug it! What do you think 5G cell towers are doing?

Dr. Fauci's involvement in the Wuhan Lab

It was uncovered that Fauci was involved in the gain of function with the Chinese Wuhan laboratory that released COVID on the world. During a Senate investigation, Dr. Anthony Fauci defended the U.S. giving hundreds of thousands of dollars for COVID research at a Wuhan lab and whether or not bat coronaviruses could be transmitted to humans, saying that it would have been "negligent" not to do so.

In 2021, Dr. Fauci said, almost prophetically, that he worried about 'unregulated' laboratories, perhaps outside of the United States, doing work 'sloppily' and leading to an inadvertent pandemic. The U.S. government and Dr. Fauci knew that viral GoF (gain of function) was concerning. Yet, he encouraged U.S. scientists to pause gain of function research but offshored the paused research to China.

Gain-of-function research (GoF research or GoFR) is medical research that genetically alters an organism in a way that may enhance the biological functions of gene products. This may include an altered pathogenesis, transmissibility, or host range, such as the types of hosts that a microorganism can infect.

More insanity: now we need to worry about the United States experimenting with COVID-19. The Economic Times recently revealed that Boston University developed a stronger COVID strain with an 80% stronger kill rate than the original COVID-19 strain. That's insanity! What if it escapes like it did in Wuhan, China in late 2019? Will it kill most of humanity worldwide?

This new strain of COVID-19 is a hybrid variety created by scientists at Boston University that is highly potent and has an 80 percent chance of death. Scientists conducted this study, but it has not gone down well with medical experts and scientists. Professor Shmuel Shapira, a leading scientist with the Israeli government, warned the scientists at Boston University not to play with fire and indulge in manipulated virus research that peers haven't monitored. Dr. Richard Ebright of Rutgers University, a leading chemist, believes that if research is carried out, it helps us understand what goes wrong. It is only then that we can avoid the next lab-generated pandemic, but that is erroneous thinking and dangerous. Why should scientists experiment with deadly viruses in the first place when there is the possibility that the virus could escape or be sabotaged and end all of humanity?

Dr. Sucharit Bhakdi, M.D. on the Damage of the Vaccine

World-renowned microbiologist and virologist professor Sucharit Bhakdi, M.D. has won many medical and scientific awards and has more than 300 peer-reviewed research papers. Dr. Bhakdi was one of the first top global doctors to warn about the debilitating effects of the CV19 vaccine. He said there is proof that if the injections reach the heart or the brain, they will be damaged beyond repair. Dr. Bhakdi brought up one autopsy and explained, "In multiple parts of the brain in this deceased man, the doctor found the same thing. He found the spike proteins in the smallest capillaries of the brain. There is no repair. Dr. Bhakdi discovered these small vessels were attacked by the immune system and destroyed. There was irrefutable evidence of brain cell damage of cells that are dead and dying. The patient had typical things now seen in people post-vax. They lose their personality. They lose their minds. They lose their capacity to think, they get dementia, they can't hear, speak, or see and they are no longer the humans that they once were. They are destroyed human beings.

What Dr. Bhakdi found was so horrible he published it on October 1, 2022, in "Vaccine," a leading scientific journal, available to the public. The doctor doing the autopsy found apart from these terrible things happening to the brain, the same conditions were happening in the heart. He discovered the same designed spike proteins. This means the gene that the perpetrators injected into billions of people reach the vessels of the brain and the heart. They are killing people in the most terrible, terrifying, and tormenting way."

Dr. Bhakdi says the world should stop the injections now—and that COVID is a "criminal hoax." He went on to say, "I am afraid to say it, but up until one and a half years ago, I was a scientist. Now, I see what is going on. I have to admit that my colleagues and friends of mine that have been telling me that this is genocide may be right. I don't know, but I feel in my mind there can be no other agenda. There is no other explanation. There is no other explanation because it is clear these gene-based vaccines are not needed because we are not dealing with a killer virus that is destroying mankind. Anyone who says otherwise is obviously lying to your face. Second, it is obvious these so-called vaccines never protected against infection. Third, and worst, these gene-based vaccines are the most terrible instruments that have ever been introduced into the human body to destroy humans. These vaccines are going to destroy mankind."

Dr. Bhakdi says the German government is persecuting him with totally false charges of antisemitism, but he is really being punished for speaking out against the CV19 vax. Early on he told people **not** to get the CV19 injections. If convicted, Dr. Bhakdi says he faces 5 years in prison. His trial is set for 2023.

We stand at a precipice of disaster where all life on Earth will end either by nuclear war or another deadly virus human-created.

Censorship for Doctors

Some doctors won't buy into censorship if they tell the truth about what is happening to people who had adverse reactions from the COVID-19 vaccines. UK's Dr. Aseem Malhotra looked into the evidence on COVID vaccines, specifically the mRNA vaccines after his father passed away suddenly after receiving the Pfizer vaccine. In his recent research paper, Dr. Malhotra, a National Health

Service (NHS) trained cardiologist, has claimed the potential harm of Pfizer's COVID vaccines and was recently banned for three weeks on Facebook. Dr. Malhotra has said that his father's rapidly progressive coronary artery disease and sudden cardiac arrest were most likely due to the mRNA product.

Of course, after Dr. Malhotra revealed his findings, the cancel culture came out in force to block him or debunk him as fake information, including Google. Even Dr. Malone, the doctor who created the mRNA technology used in some coronavirus vaccines says he was censored by YouTube for sharing his concerns about the vaccine. He said, "One of my concerns is that the government is not being transparent with us about what those risks are. And so, I'm of the opinion that people have the right to decide whether to accept a vaccine or not, especially since these are experimental vaccines."

COVID-19 vaccine turns negative in months

The negative reports just keep coming, but everyone needs to know the truth. The effectiveness of the Pfizer and AstraZeneca COVID-19 vaccines turn negative against severe COVID-19 months after administration, according to a new study. The negative effectiveness estimates in the study indicate that vaccinated people are more likely to experience severe COVID-19 than unvaccinated people. A single dose of the AstraZeneca vaccine turned negative at day 70 and a second dose turned negative at day 84, according to the paper, which was published in the International Journal of Epidemiology.

So, my friends, we have all been hoodwinked by the Family of Dark again. We are controlled like sheep in a pen by those who think they own us—from the government to the World Management Team to those beings in space. The greatest tyranny in our world is not controlled by martial law, but through psychological manipulation of consciousness — frequency. You are in an invisible prison, and you do not realize that there is something outside it.

Because people in the United States and throughout the world are so frightened of giving up the system, they are going to be forced to give it up. The system is corrupt and out of balance and does not work, it does not honor life, and it does not honor Earth. If something does not honor life and does not honor Mother Earth, you can bet it is going to fall big time.

Consciousness must change even if it takes something so huge and destructive to awaken humans, and I am afraid that is what will happen soon. People will stand up once they have lost everything in life. Humans have lost their morality, their spiritualism, and their faith in God and life. People will be forced to awaken.

COVID was meant to remove most of the Earth's inhabitants. In the book, *The Watchers II*, by Raymond E. Fowler, Betty Andreasson Luca was told by the extraterrestrials that she had encountered most of her life that "They keep seed from man and woman so the human form will not be lost." The Gray Watchers (mature human fetuses) claim that they are being used to assure that human and natural forms will not be lost. Betty was also told that the toxins we have created will render humans sterile in the future.

Is the government responsible for Cattle Mutilations?

I began investigating the cattle mutilation taking place across the country in late 1970 while living in Idaho. I contacted renowned cattle mutilation investigator Tom Adams and began collaborating with him on Idaho mutilations reported by local ranchers. Cattle mute investigator Tom Adams reported that ranchers had noted that numbers of the dead animals had infrared markers on their backs, visible only at night with special night vision, meaning animals had been preselected before they were killed.

Another source emerged in the La Grande Observer when a private citizen who wished to be anonymous told their reporter, "We know the government is experimenting with a war weapon."

He went on to say it involves an ultra-sound 1 ½-inch shock wave, and when directed into the animal, breaks down the cell walls and the cellular contents. If true, it could certainly account for the mutilations taking place close to U.S. military bases.

By 1980, news reporter and earth mysteries investigator Linda Moulton Howe, a Boise, Idaho native, became well-known for her cattle mutilation investigations while working at KMGH-TV in Denver, Colorado, which won Howe an Emmy. She concluded after interviewing countless ranchers that their testimony suggested the presence of extraterrestrial mutilators. She and other UFO investigators believed the federal government knew who was behind the mutilations and have aggressively covered up the truth for decades. Howe discovered the mutilations weren't contained to only the United States but had taken place in Canada, Puerto Rico, Panama, the Canary Islands, and other South American and European countries. No country, it seemed, had been spared the grisly mutilations.

As Tom Adams explained the real victims were the ranchers and farmers who reported mutilations to law enforcement bodies and/or the press, not out of a civic "duty" but for a real desire to learn who was responsible for these heinous acts. But once the mutilation was reported, little or nothing could be done without the perpetrator or perpetrators being apprehended. In the beginning, a few sheriffs and law enforcement were enthusiastic about investigating the cases, but soon their enthusiasm waned with the inability to obtain substantive evidence. There was also the mockery to contend with from their peers who joked aliens had a new appetite for beef.

After years of logged-in calls, sheriffs across the country refused to investigate mutilations altogether, and soon livestock owners stopped reporting their dead cattle, knowing it was futile. It seemed both law enforcement agencies and ranchers didn't want the publicity and ridicule. If it wasn't for investigative reporters like Linda Moulton Howe producing award-winning documentaries, the cattle mutilation phenomena would have been ignored entirely by the news media.

Some felt that Howe's book, *An Alien Harvest*, leaned too heavily on the UFO/mute link instead of pursuing other evidence that might have offered a more earthly explanation. After a decade of research on the continuing cattle mutilations across the United States, Howe concluded from an accumulation of human testimony, it suggested the presence of extraterrestrial mutilators. She and other UFO investigators also believed the federal government has known of these killings and had aggressively created a massive cover-up for decades. Howe believes it's one of the best-kept secrets of our time.

Through the Freedom of Information Act, Howe obtained documents showing cattle mutilations and UFO sightings dating back to 1947 near Emmett, Idaho. The government had previously denied conducting these investigations. Hundreds of thousands of mutilations have taken place around the world since the sixties. The headlines first hit the news in the West by the 1970s when 90 cases alone were reported in Idaho. Other investigators, unlike law enforcement's theories of predators, cults, and natural causes, disregarded extraterrestrials and UFOs and took an earthlier explanation pointing to a federal agency behind the activity, especially in light of helicopter sightings, known surgical procedures, detected traces of known germ warfare toxins, and the financial resources necessary to support such an operation.

The proof of such operations occurred in 1968 when six thousand sheep suddenly dropped dead in Northern Utah, traced back to the U.S. Army installation Dugway Proving Grounds, a biological warfare research center operated by the Feds, 85 miles southwest of Salt Lake City. Dugway had accidentally released a deadly VX gas causing the massive killing of sheep. The outcry from citizens was so great after the incident, President Nixon ordered an immediate halt to any further research in germ warfare and the destruction of existing stockpiles at Dugway.

Dugway Proving Grounds is a facility in service to all branches of the U.S. military. By 1975, Senator Frank Church's Senate Select Subcommittee on Intelligence discovered that not all the toxic material had been destroyed. It seems the CIA had stored large quantities of various toxic chemicals at several locations and traces of one of these deadly toxins produced by the Clostridia genus were detected in many of the mutilated cattle. Isn't that a frightening revelation?

Dugway Installation is the size of Rhode Island and is strategically surrounded by three massive mountain ranges. Its size and remote isolation make it an ideal location for secret testing like another infamous installation—Area 51 near Las Vegas, Nevada. There's speculation that Dugway has tested the applications and effects of every known biological, chemical, and radiological substance on earth. There is a long history of concerned locals that military testing of deadly agents is extremely harmful to humans, animals, and the environment.

On January 26, 2011, a local Utah television station reported on the sudden shutdown of all operations at Dugway and on the simultaneous lockdown of everyone who worked there. The facility was put under lockdown due to the loss of an "extremely toxic nerve agent" according to an "official" report. But at the same time UFOs were sighted and photographed around Dugway by credible witnesses.

Unusual craft has been seen zipping through the skies over and around the Dugway installations for many years, apparently concerned about the clandestine activities there. A Utah television station reported UFO sightings by two witnesses that occurred close to the time Dugway had its lockdown. There was film footage of strange light-formations that made unusual maneuvers near the base. Dugway closed shortly after the lights appeared. Coincidence? Not likely!

Perhaps the increased UFO activity would explain the need for aliens to dissect different species of animals in different climates and geography worldwide to determine what our military is doing to our cattle, humanity, and our environment.

Cattle mute investigator Tom Adams said that ranchers had noted that numbers of the dead animals had infrared markers on their backs, visible only at night with special night vision, meaning animals had been preselected before they were killed. Another source emerged in the La Grande Observer when a private citizen who wished to be anonymous told their reporter, "We know the government is experimenting with a war weapon." He went on to say it involves an ultra-sound 1 ½-inch shock wave, and when directed into the animal, breaks down the cell walls and the cellular contents. If this is true, it could certainly account for the mutilations taking place close to U.S. military bases.

No matter where the mutilations take place, the scenario usually was disturbingly the same; blood was drained completely from the animal, and there were never any footprints or tracks of any kind near the carcass. Organs removed from the animals consisted of sense organs, sexual organs, organs associated with the digestion and elimination process, and in some cases, the heart, liver, and kidneys. There had been cases where the flesh was stripped from one side of the jaw. But the strangest scenario in most cases was the absence of blood in the animals—or blood on the ground or near the carcass. With the wounds mentioned above, these animals should have bled profusely, but don't, not in the place where they were discovered. Then there is the absence of human, predator, or vehicle tracks in mud, snow, and grass. Another interesting note-- many of the animals had broken bones as if they were dropped from a great height.

Linda Moulton Howe was able to take many samples to the University of Colorado's Medical Center where they concluded the mutilations were done by a pinpoint heat source, which took an estimated two minutes. Possibly a laser—but remember during the sixties and seventies' laser technology was still in its infancy and lasers weighed approximately 550 pounds. It would have been unconscionable for a helicopter to transport a large cow to another location, do its evil deed with a large laser, and then drop the cow back in another location within minutes. I say minutes because many of the mutilations have taken place within a short time, only a few yards from a farmhouse according to many reliable reports from farmers and ranchers.

Another confirmation of the possible laser technology used on cattle came from Linda Moulton Howe's contact Dr. Arlen Meyers, an expert laser surgeon at Rose Medical Center in Denver. He believed after examining cattle mutilation photographs that it appeared the mutilations could be created by a burning or laser-type instrument, but he felt that to bring such a device to a remote area and inflict that sort of damage on a piece of livestock would be extremely difficult.

Investigators in Idaho and Colorado concluded the deaths were by natural causes or predators, but it was noted that in most cases natural predators, including birds, would not go near the carcass. Even dogs had the hackles on their backs raised when they went near the dead animal. Law enforcement agencies I spoke to during the 1970s into the early 1980s were hesitant to discuss the mutilations, but usually suggested natural predators, lightning and cults were to blame. Sheriff Brent in Bear Lake County on the Idaho/Utah border said there had been 14 mutilations at that time, including an 8-month-old heifer calf with its ear, anus, udder, and tongue missing. He added that UFO lights were seen in the area.

In 1980, an ex-FBI agent named Kenneth Rommel was hired by the federal government to investigate the mutilation cases, which became a 300-page report. He concluded in his report that most of the deaths were of a natural origin done by predators and scavengers, and in the few cases where human involvement was determined, the culprits were not highly sophisticated "surgeons" but pranksters, publicity seekers, and other ordinary individuals, and he had several state diagnostic laboratories to back up his report. Rommel's findings compared to those of other law enforcement officials and veterinarians. Howe angrily dismissed Rommel's report as a cover-up that didn't even deal with real cases.

Linda Moulton Howe gathered pages of interviews from eyewitnesses and government officials who told her incredible stories, despite their fear of retribution. Some claimed they had taken oaths of secrecy and would go to jail without a trial if they talked. By 1983, Howe was taken to a secure room at Kirtland Air Force Base in Albuquerque, New Mexico by an Air Force investigator. Inside the room, she was shown a document titled, "Briefing Paper for the President of the United States of America."

The paper revealed UFO sightings that go back tens of thousands of years and claimed DNA manipulation of Earth's primates. The paper went on to reveal the 1940s UFO crashes with details of live and dead aliens recovered by the government.

In Brazil, cattle mutilations became a hotbed of activity during the 1970s. On October 27, 1970, towards the end of the afternoon under a cloudy sky. Pedro Trajano Machado, age sixty-six, and his twenty-three-year-old son, Euripides de Jesus Trindade, were on their farm about 15 miles from Palma (in the Alegrete area, again in the state of Rio Grande do Sul) taking care of some cattle. They had shut up 18 head of cows in a corral and separated a red Jersey Cow from her month-old calf, which weighed about 60 pounds. The cow was led off to be worked and her calf was left loose to roam the corral about fifteen feet from where Pedro and his son worked.

They suddenly noticed that the other cattle had become quite nervous and upset, especially the red cow. At first, they didn't pay attention to this, but as a little more time went by the herd became extremely agitated. The red cow began bellowing as if something was horribly wrong and kept trying to turn her head to look in the direction of her calf. Pedro decided to see what was wrong with the calf. The cow spotted the calf bawling at this point, but it wasn't on the ground. Instead, the calf was suspended about three feet in the air, in its normal position, not tipped over one way or the other. Pedro called to his son and they both watched in paralyzed terror. The calf was being moved parallel to the ground at the same height of about three feet in the direction of the fields, while the other animals bellowed.

The two witnesses remained rooted to the ground, watching this unbelievable event, incapable of taking action as the calf moved along at least sixty feet and then began to rise vertically, so slowly that it took three or four minutes before it was so high in the sky as to look about a quarter of its original size before vanishing from sight. Oddly, the calf stopped bawling as it started to rise. No other phenomenon was reported. The calf simply vanished and was never seen again.

The reason I bring up cattle mutilations is that I believe our military or government has been developing biological agents and using ranchers' cattle for their experimentation. I also believe that aliens have colluded with the military in many of the mutilations especially when unmarked black helicopters are seen either before or after the mutilation of the cow takes place. The helicopters are silent.

Some investigators feel there is a link to the helicopters and certain military bases in the southwest. It was rumored in the mid-1970s that the military was conducting a UFO investigation from a secret installation on either Fort Hood or Gary Air Force Base located in Killeen, Texas, near the AEC's Killeen Base, one of three National Stockpile sites where nuclear weapons were stored at the time.

Reports within the affected ranching communities indicated that the mutilations regularly coincided with the sighting of mysterious unmarked helicopters. Some ranchers who suffered the worst losses believed the federal government had performed the mutilations—for an assortment of reasons, including the testing of biological weaponry. Animosity for the government proved so heated that the Nebraska National Guard ordered their helicopters to cruise at 2,000 feet (rather than the regular 1,000-foot altitude), for their safety, since panicky ranchers had begun shooting at helicopters.

Investigators have discovered strap marks, bruises, broken bones, and steer horns embedded in the ground indicating the animals were transported by air to another location, mutilated, and then returned to another location, away from the original location pickup. In some cases, legs were broken where it appeared that clamping devices had been attached to airlift the animal, perhaps to nearby military bases. A clamping device sounds more like human perpetrators than advanced alien technology.

Although cattle mutilations peaked in the 1970s into the 1990s, cattle mutilations continue.

Just think of the billions of dollars such a clandestine operation would take without Congressional approval. And the biggest question is why? Some conspiracy theorists suspect certain pathogens have been introduced to our environment, such as HIV, Mad Cow Disease, West Nile Virus, and perhaps even COVID. Have you ever questioned how COVID traveled around the world and affect people in some of the most remote places within a very short time?

You probably dismiss such conspiracy theories, but here is hard evidence that our government has conducted horrible experiments on people without their consent.

In 1931 when Dr. Cornelius Rhoads, under the auspices of the Rockefeller Institute for Medical Investigations, infected human subjects with cancer cells. He later went on to establish the U.S. Army Biological Warfare facilities in Maryland, Utah, and Panama. While there, he began a series of radiation exposure experiments on American soldiers and civilian hospital patients without their knowledge.

In 1932 the Tuskegee Syphilis Study began using 200 black men diagnosed with syphilis. They were denied treatment, serving as guinea pigs while the disease progressed, and subsequently, they died from the disease. Their families were never told that they could have been treated and cured.

From 1942 to 1945 Chemical Warfare Services started mustard gas experiments on approximately 4,000 servicemen. By 1944 the U.S. Navy used human subjects to test gas masks and clothing by locking individuals in a gas chamber and exposing them to mustard gas and lewisite, an organoarsenic compound manufactured in the U.S. and Japan as a chemical weapon. In 1945 "Program F" was implemented by the U.S. Atomic Energy Commission to test the health effects of fluoride, which was the key chemical component in atomic bomb production. Fluoride is one of the most toxic chemicals known to man and has been known to cause adverse effects on the central nervous system. Much of the information was hushed up in the name of national security because of the fear that lawsuits would undermine the full-scale production of atomic bombs.

Did you know that fluoride is added to most drinking water across the United States with many environmental and health-conscious groups trying to ban its use? Further studies have shown IQ impairment both in learning and memory among the fluoride-treated groups and IQ deficits in children. It indicates damage to the central nervous system and the brain. Again, it seems the cattle mutilation operation has insidious overtones that we are being used as guinea pigs for a variety of toxic chemicals testing.

In 1947 Colonel E. E. Kirkpatrick of the U.S. Atomic Energy Commission issued a secret document (Document 07075001, January 8, 1947) stating that the agency would begin administering intravenous doses of radioactive substances to human subjects. During the same year, the CIA began studying LSD as a potential weapon for use by American intelligence. Human subjects, both civilian and military, were used as test subjects with and without their knowledge.

By 1950 the Department of Defense was implementing plans to detonate nuclear weapons in desert areas (above ground) and monitor residents in the area for medical problems and mortality rates. Propaganda movies showed the military without protective gear watching an atomic bomb blast nearby, and of course, many movies were made shortly after these areas were blasted, which contained high levels of radiation. Actors like John Wayne, diagnosed with stomach cancer in the late seventies, and many others may have paid dearly with their health years later while working in those bomb site areas. 1950 was the same year the U.S. Navy sprayed a cloud of bacteria from ships over San Francisco to find out how susceptible an American City would be to a biological attack. Yes, the U.S. Military was experimenting on their citizens! Many people became ill with pneumonia-like symptoms.

From 1953 to 1958, there were more tests of zinc cadmium sulfide gas released over Winnipeg, St. Louis, Minneapolis, Fort Wayne, Maryland, and Virginia. Not only were biological agents and chemicals being tested, but projects like MK ULTRA and Project Monarch were conducted using drugs and biological agents to be used for mind control on unwitting adults and children.

Through the years the military's nefarious deeds and testing didn't stop. In 1968, the CIA experimented with the possibility of poisoning drinking water by injecting chemicals into the water supply of the FDA in Washington, D.C. 1968 was the same year that Dugway Proving Military Installation in northwestern Utah released the VX gas, killing six thousand sheep.

The military has little concern for its citizens as their criminal experiments continue. There's little doubt that AIDS erupted in the U.S. shortly after government-sponsored hepatitis B vaccine experiments were initiated on gay men as guinea pigs from 1978 to 1981. The epidemic was caused by a new retrovirus (the human virus or HIV); and the introduction of a new herpes-8 virus which causes Kaposi's sarcoma, known as the "gay cancer" of AIDS.

Reports claimed that HIV/AIDS originated in a monkey or chimpanzee virus that "jumped species" in Africa. However, the first AIDS cases were first reported in gay men in Manhattan in 1978, four years before the epidemic was first noticed in Africa. It's incomprehensible how two African species-jumping viruses ended up exclusively in gay men in Manhattan during the late Seventies. There is further speculation by researchers who believe that AIDS is a man-made virus and that two primate viruses were introduced and spread during the government's recruitment of thousands of male homosexuals beginning in 1974.

During the Gulf War's Desert Storm Operation soldiers began complaining about mysterious ailments. Dr. Garth Nicolson at the MD Anderson Cancer Center in Houston, Texas discovered that these soldiers were infected with an altered strain of Mycoplasma Incognitus, a microbe commonly used in the production of biological weapons. Tests confirmed that the molecular structure was man-made. Courageous men and women who served in Desert Storm are still suffering, and our government won't admit they were exposed to toxic chemical agents so they can be compensated and treated.

Here's another example of the U.S. military/government conducting experiments on the public without their knowledge. Between 1929 and 1974, it is estimated 65,000 were victims of forced sterilization in at least 30 states, and nearly 7,600 people were sterilized under the orders from North Carolina's Eugenics Board. Nearly 85 percent were women and young girls, as young as 10. Now North Carolina is offering to compensate the victims with fifty thousand dollars, shut-up money, they say. How can money restore a body part and their dignity? What other monstrous experiments have gone on through the years we don't even know about? This is just a small list of all the clandestine tests that have been performed on citizens around the world. Is it any wonder we don't trust our leaders and government officials? How many more tests have been or are currently being tested on us, and this includes the cattle mutilations or as it is sometimes referred to as "Mutegate"?

So, I ask each of you, do you really believe that COVID was accidentally released from the Wuhan Laboratory in China? Do you think that they wanted to stop COVID with experimental vaccines by various pharmaceutical companies? It was a heinous experiment on humanity, and you were the guinea pigs. Have you noticed how people have changed that took the vaccine? They don't think straight, and many have become mean-spirited humans. A number of my clients have mentioned this to me. Again, I wonder if human DNA was altered, and for what evil purpose? No doubt the dark reason for the experimental vaccines will become known in the future.

This is just the beginning of their plan for total control of the planet, as they get richer from human suffering. Deception is an old tool that is only effective because you choose denial rather than facing the implications of what is obvious. Awareness is an all-empowering device to recognize ignorance. If you trust your feelings and your innate sixth sense, then you will know the truth from falsehood. Unfortunately, many people never fully realize the disinformation presented daily that pushes them away from the bigger picture of reality.

How far must the lies be pushed on humanity before humans awaken? You are in a test about reality and how you will reject or buy into the fear. Will you continue to believe what is written in newspapers and told on certain television stations to control you?

Once upon a time journalists investigated a story to get to the truth and prove accurate information. That is no longer true in most cases. Have you noticed how certain newscasters repeat certain words over and over?

CHAPTER THREE

Save the Children

Marvin Gaye (1939-1984) wrote several ecology songs during the 1970s, *What's Going On, Mercy, Mercy Me*, and the hit song *Save the Children*. Read the lyrics to *Save the Children* below and how they resonate in today's world:

I just want to ask a question: Who really cares, to save a world in despair?
Who really cares? (Ohhh)
There'll come a time (There'll come a time)
When the world won't be singing (When the world won't be singing)
Flowers won't grow (Flowers won't grow, no)
Bells won't be ringin' (The bells won't be ringin')
Who really cares? (Who really cares?)
Who's willing to try? (Who is willin' to try?)

To save the world (To save the world)
That's destined to die (That is destined to die)
When I look at the world (When I look at the world)
It fills me with sorrow (It fills me with sorrow)
Little children today (Children today)
Are really gonna suffer tomorrow (Really suffer tomorrow)
(Oh!) What a shame (What a shame)
Such a bad way to live (Such a bad way to live)
Oh, who is to blame? (Who is to blame?)
We can't stop living (When we can't stop living)
(Ohhh!) Live, (Live)
(Live for life) Live for life
(But let live everybody)
Live life for the children (Live life for the children!)
(Oh, for the Children!)
You see, let's... (Oh!) let's save the children (Oh)
Let's...let's save all the children
(Save the babies! Save the babies!)
(And if you want to love, you got to save the babies!)
(Oh you've got the feeling, you've got the feeling)
(You will save the babies! All of the children of the world!)

Scientists say that sperm counts are down in men and women are miscarrying. Scientists searching for the causes of falling sperm counts are getting a clearer picture of the role played by chemical pollutants - and it's not a pretty one. A study of urine samples from nearly 100 male volunteers has uncovered "alarming" levels of endocrine disruptors known to reduce human fertility. Cocktails of chemicals such as bisphenols and dioxins, which are believed to interfere with hormones and affect sperm quality, were present at levels up to 100 times those considered safe. The median exposure to these chemicals was 17 times the levels deemed acceptable.

The scientists were also surprised to find that bisphenol A (BPA) was the dominant risk factor, given that recent research had focused on phthalates, which are used in plastics. BPA was followed by dioxins, paracetamol, and phthalates. Removing BPA from the mix did not bring down the combined exposure to acceptable levels, and paracetamol was described as "a driver of mixture risks among subjects using the drug." Another uncertainty is whether women of reproductive age have the same levels of chemical exposure as the men in the study.

But the researchers stressed their research may underestimate the risk posed by exposure to these chemical cocktails, given "the multitude of chemicals humans are exposed to" — which were not all measured in this study. We are killing life by the toxins in our environment and by abortion.

In the book, *Memories of Heaven*, by Dr. Wayne W. Dyer and Dee Garnes, they wrote true stories of children mailed to them by parents across the U.S. and Canada, who recalled watching their parents from Heaven before they were born and describing everything they were doing at the time. Babies are old souls that need to come back to evolve spiritually and with lessons unlearned from past lives. We are harming the cycle of rebirth.

Dr. Dyer wrote, "In the New Testament, Jesus tells us, 'The 'light of the body is the eye' if therefore thine eye be single, thy whole body shall be full of light." (Matthew 6:22). This means that when we use our human eyes to see only Oneness, rather than all of the dualities that make for conflict, sadness and pain, we are experiencing what heaven is really like."

We have forgotten the Oneness of everything and how God's light shines in everyone, including those who do evil. Their souls before arriving on this planet were pure until they decided to harm others.

Migrant Children and Biden's Administration

It is estimated that over 4 to 5 million migrants have crossed the United States borders in the past few years. A large number are unaccompanied children. The Biden administration has lost track of nearly 20,000 kids. Children are flown or on charter buses in the middle of the night to New York City and other major cities and then sent to unvetted sponsors, and no one in authority can verify who these sponsors are. Sex trafficking is happening worldwide in major countries and through the Mexican cartel. Two to three hundred children are moved at a time on one chartered plane, according to an anonymous whistleblower working for MVM Inc., a federally funded company, that has been involved with moving 8,000 to 10,000 kids weekly. Where are the kids sent and with whom? Cartels?

There aren't enough sponsors or foster parents to take them at that rate, so the question is who is taking these young children and for what reason. Some claim they are friends, but that's not always true. Anyone who shows up or claims they are a relative or has documentation can take the child or children. At the beginning of the program, family members claimed the children, but no more. Family members would hug and cry seeing their kids, but not the people who are claiming them now. That has all changed. Children are upset with these strangers taking them. Sponsors are getting up to $2000 or more from federal contractors.

Can you imagine how many of these kids are going to be abused by sick demented people? They are falling into the governmental cracks, and nothing can be done to save them. This is all funded by American taxpayers.

The whistleblower said the Biden Administration has made this a huge mess.

Woke Schools

Our precious children lost two years in school learning from the COVID-19 lockdowns. The ramifications of this unnecessary act will cause a generation of psychological problems, depression, and mistrust of adults and the government system. When the mask mandates were forced on children, they wore masks in schools for hours. Can you imagine what it did when they weren't getting enough oxygen in their lungs and brains? And we wonder why the United States has some of the lowest scores in reading and math in the world.

What were the officials thinking when they made these mandates? And the weird part is that children were more immune to COVID than adults and senior adults. Yet, they were treated like lepers like the rest of the world. We were told it was a virus of the unvaccinated, and in truth, it was a virus of the vaccinated. It's been proven that vaccines didn't stop the transmission of the disease as they promised. It was never meant to do that, but they (CDC and other officials) told us it would. We were hoodwinked.

More people caught the virus who were vaccinated, than those who weren't. President Joe Biden caught COVID-19 twice, and his cabinet also tested positive—Press Secretary Karine Jean-Pierre, Interior Secretary Deb Haaland, Vice President Kamala Harris, Attorney General Merrick Garland, Agriculture Secretary Tom Visack, Commerce Secretary Gina Raimondo, Secretary of State Antony Blinken, Secretary of Health and Human Services Xavier Becerra and several others. Both Dr. Anthony Fauci, the one who claimed to follow the science, tested positive for COVID in June of 2022, as well as CDC Director Dr. Rochelle Walensky.

Then there are the woke ideologies or should I say propaganda being waged on school children on the Critical Race Theory (CTR), which has been taught to school children in secret to hate their parents and hate white people. It's a divisive discourse that pits people of color against white people. But that's not the worst of it— certain teachers began pushing gender transition to children. Explicit sex manuals were being taught to young children without their parent's permission. I have nothing against transexuals, but visiting school rooms and restaurants is asinine and doing their sexual dances in front of small children is insane.

Here's more insanity—schools allow biological males dressed as women in school locker rooms who can compete as a female in girls' sports. There's also been rape. In Loudoun County, Virginia last year a transgender teenager sexually raped a 15-year-old female student in the school bathroom. This case galvanized parents fighting against woke school boards. The father of the young girl was arrested for speaking out in school about his daughter's rape and the school board did nothing, claiming there was no assault. The boy involved was sent to another school and was never punished. The girl's father, Scott Smith, was treated worse than the attacker by the school system.

Our children need to enjoy what little fleeting time they have in childhood, and they don't need adults pushing them into sex, pornography, and transgenderism.

Remember when Ketanji Brown Jackson's Supreme Court was going through her confirmation for Supreme Court Justice? Sen. Marsha Blackburn (R-Tenn.) asked, "Can you provide a definition for the word 'woman'?" as she questioned Jackson about a transgender athlete. "Can I provide a definition? No. I can't," responded Jackson. And then she said added, "I'm not a biologist."

But Ms. Blackburn pressed the point. "The fact that you can't give me a straight answer about something as fundamental as what a woman underscores the dangers of the kind of progressive education that we are hearing about," she said. "Just last week, an entire generation of young girls watched as our taxpayer-funded institutions permitted a biological man to compete and be a biological woman in the N.C.A.A. swimming championships. What message do you think this sends to girls who aspire to compete and win in sports at the highest levels?"

Do we all need to become biologists to know what a woman is? The answer is simple, you can change your body, but you can't change your chromosomes. Females have two X chromosomes, while males have one X and one Y chromosome. It's not fair that a biological male can compete in women's sports.

And then there's the insanity of teachers pushing transgenderism on young children and giving them sexual manuals to look at without the parents' permission. Why are children as young as fifteen years old having body parts removed and taking puberty blockers? They can do whatever they want when they become an adult, but children are still growing, and most young children under eighteen don't know what they want.

Parents who try to do something about woke propaganda being taught in schools are arrested and put in jail. Our government and our school unions can do what they want with your children, and parents can't do anything about it. This is pure Draconian and it's going to get worse if we don't act. We are going to repeat the Nazi horrors of World War II.

In World War II, Adolf Hitler believed that securing the loyalty and obedience of children was essential if Nazism was to survive beyond the current generation. Consequently, children in Nazi Germany were subjected to intensive propaganda through mediums of education, training, and social groups. That is what we are seeing with young children in schools across the country taught woke propaganda. Children are old souls in young bodies. They need the opportunity to evolve mentally, spiritually, and physically. Religion and God has been removed from many aspects of life. Children today are programmed to be unemotional. There are millions of children that recall past lives, see spirits, and are psychic and telepathic, but they have no one to help them prepare for their special gifts. Most parents don't want to deal with psychic children. They are either frightened of their gifts or don't know how to help them. They need guidance so their gifts are channels in dark ways. It's up to parents to help them—learn about metaphysics, reincarnation, and telepathic children. They are here to help us evolve.

Books are being banned. Obama wants you to believe the Republicans are going to burn books, but in truth, Democrats have banned classic children's books because of wokism like *Dr. Seuss, Winnie the Pooh, Charlotte's Web, Peter Pan,* Mark Twain's book, *The Adventure of Huckleberry Finn, Where's Waldo* and many more beloved classics.

Have you noticed how the Democratic Left plays a child's game of opposite day? Whatever the Republicans say about them, the Democrats repeat the same rhetoric. You are told that you are going to live in Nazi Ville if you vote Republican, that your social security will be taken from you, and on and on…and that Republicans will control the world with their socialism. This is mind control 101. I've never seen such hypocrisy from Barack Obama, Joe Biden, and the rest of the knuckleheads out there.

Prophecy Now

CHAPTER FOUR

California Lost

In 1967, I moved to Southern California from Idaho and fell in love with the weather, the ocean, the smell of the Eucalyptus trees by the ocean on a foggy day, the new age bookstores, and spiritual people and retreats. It was good vibrations. I worked at brokerage firms in Beverly Hills for many years and met many celebrities. During the early 1980s, I volunteered at Stephan A. Schwartz's Mobius Group, a foundation that explored remote viewing, psychic abilities, and psychic archaeology, and later worked for the Disney Channel and Disney Real Estate department in Burbank.

My former husband was an architectural model maker with a business in downtown Los Angeles in a loft studio. Everywhere homeless people lived in the streets. We often gave money to the homeless, but that stopped when we learned they were robbed and between. It was bad then and it's ten times worse now. The homeless live in Beverly Hills and on the beaches in tents. They do drugs, and defecate on the streets and beaches.

In 1987, my former husband and I moved to Sonoma in Northern California. We visited my husband's family in San Francisco, and I remember seeing homeless people camped along the streets and human feces everywhere. It was that bad in 1987.

Now California's tyrannical Governor Newsom wants to control what doctors tell their patients. Physicians will no longer have freedom of speech as of January 1, 2023, per Governor Newsom. Doesn't this sound like a dictator? Critics of the law, including many mainstream doctors who have advocated passionately for masks and vaccines, say it could end up curbing well-intentioned conversations between patients and physicians about a disease that's still changing from one month to the next. California doctors will soon be subject to disciplinary action if they give their patients information about COVID-19 that they know to be false or misleading. This measure was signed by Gov. Gavin Newsom and goes into effect on Jan. 1, 2023.

It's ludicrous that Gavin Newsom pushes millions of Californians and small children to have the COVID vaccine, an experimental drug, but when people began to have amazing results from Ivermectin, a drug that cost very little, it was condemned as a horse dewormer, and dangerous for human use. The claim was completely false.

Besides what Newsom plans to do to fossil fuels in the near future, Californians deal with rising crime in a sanctuary state where any illegal migrant, criminal, or drug cartel can live. Did you know that in Northern California there are huge marijuana farms grown by the cartel and our law enforcement can't touch them? In San Francisco, any drug is legal and can be bought and taken on the street. People are fleeing that once beautiful city on the bay because of the homeless situation, crime, and drugs on the streets.

Even Newsom's in-laws, Republicans, decided to move from California to Florida to escape him. Governor Newsom is unhinged!

Governor Gavin Newsom. a Libra, born on October 10, 1967, has four children. You'd think that Newsom would be concerned about his own children growing up in a sanctuary state where drugs and crime are out of control. California has adopted many aspects of CRT at all levels of education. In March 2021, the state Board of Education passed an ethnic studies curriculum based in large part on CRT (Critical Race Theory) that applies to all public schools.

However, things are changing in California. On April 7, 2022, the Placentia-Yorba Linda School Board voted Tuesday night to ban the teaching of critical race theory in its classrooms, the first school district in Orange County to enact such a rule. The resolution states that the district "will not include Critical Race Theory as a framework in any course offerings" and passed by a 3-2 vote, at least momentarily ending a fiery debate about race, academic freedom, and parental control of education that has embroiled the district for months. The academic concept of CTR is a framework for teaching how racism has been historically embedded in institutions and policies.

Will Gavin Newsom run for President in 2024?

Democratic Governor Gavin Newsom paid for billboard banners in Mississippi, Texas, and several other Republican-run states in the lead-up to the November 8 midterm elections. His ads have also run-on TV against Ron DeSantis and have challenged him to a nationally televised debate. Why in 2022 or 20223? Governor DeSantis is not running against Newsom, not yet. Not unless both men run for president. Newsom claims he's not running for president, but don't believe it. He has his eyes on the White House and he already made a test run when Joe Biden was out of town and he made an unscheduled appearance to see first lady Jill Biden with his sleeves rolled up. Talk about audacious!

Governor Newsom will run in 2024 but won't get far in the presidential race. If he can't govern California, he certainly can't run the United States of America as President.

CHAPTER FIVE

Hidden Knowledge

Arcane knowledge has been hidden from humanity for thousands of years. In your awakening process, there will be a flood of endless questions about your reality and how you fit into it. Questions are wise and healthy because it opens the conditioned mindset that has been used to exploit your understanding of everything that has been erroneously told to you. A questioning mind will have a tsunami impact on mass consciousness, and your thoughts coalesce into physical reality and like seeds thrown to the wind that take root, they will grow and extend beyond borders and restraints.

For eons, humanity has been mind-controlled. Our controllers know how gullible humanity is and they use it against us with repetitive words. We always imagine a hypnotist waving an object on a necklace in front of the patient, but that isn't how it works. You see mind-control every day on television and radio with repetitive ads to make you want that product or drug. I worked for BBDO West in West Los Angles during the 1980s and I know how it works. This subliminal reinforcement is used by leaders, the military, and the Illuminati to control us. And it works well.

Even though the so-called versions of reality are being questioned, technology is a big part of what controls us. Most people use Facebook, Twitter, Tik Tok, and Instagram but there are subliminal messages in these social media programs that you are not aware of and certainly not your children. Humanity has been conditioned to believe that education institutions, and especially sciences, strive to elevate our standard of living—cell phones, the internet, and social media. Yet this is hardly the case.

Most of the worthy discoveries have been selectively hidden from the masses—independent inventors have never seen their inventions in the light of day involving alternative energy sources and health miracles. Why? Because the rich and powerful want us to believe we have no other sources of energy except their Green Deal of solar panels, electricity, and wind turbines. Most of the incredible inventors have been harassed and silenced when they explore alternative energy sources, and even those in the health fields are often threatened or killed when they discover inexpensive cures (Ivermectin for COVID) for disease. Also, geologists, journalists, and archaeologists who try to give us the truth are targeted when they present information that runs counter to the "official version" of history.

Earth is far more ancient than anyone dares to say and so is humanity. We didn't just show up 300,000 years ago. Modern humans aren't the most sophisticated or intelligent race in the solar system, which I have written about in many of my books. The moon, Mars, and even the vestiges of great ancient civilizations exist throughout the world. We, humans, are not at the top of the evolutionary ladder, yet for millennia only certain people have been privy to the secret that a wide variety of intelligent life forms have always shared Earth with us.

But more than 100 years ago, Nikola Tesla (1856-1943) invented alternating current (AC), the polyphase alternating current system, which laid the foundation for today's mass-produced power supply. From the invention of the particle beam to radar, the electric car, robotics, and remote-controlled drones, Tesla had mental-modeled solutions to problems with such clarity of mind that he could visualize the individual parts of a machine or mechanism in three dimensions. Then run simulations in his head and check for wear and tear. He even pioneered interplanetary radio communication with Guglielmo Marconi. He later had problems when the US Patent Office mysteriously overturned his patents and effectively credited Marconi with the invention of the radio, who was, in fact, using several of Tesla's patents.

Tesla was so far ahead of his time, the genius of many of his early inventions—used to develop the radio and television, fluorescent and induction lighting, and MRIs and X-rays only came to light after his death. Tesla's long-held dream was to create a source of inexhaustible, clean energy that was free for everyone. He strongly opposed centralized coal-fired power stations that spewed carbon dioxide into the air that humans breathed. He believed that the Earth had "fluid electrical charges" running beneath its surface, that when interrupted by a series of electrical discharges at repeated set intervals, would generate a limitless power supply by generating immense low-frequency electrical waves.

One of Tesla's most extraordinary experiments was to transmit electrical power over long distances without wires or cables, a feat that has baffled scientists ever since. His grand vision was to free humankind from the burdens of extracting, pumping, transporting, and burning fossil fuels—which he viewed as "sinful waste."

Tesla was eventually discouraged by what he called "ignorant, unimaginative people (Westinghouse, Edison, and JP Morgan), consumed by self-interest." Those powerful men sought to protect the immensely profitable, low-tech industries they had spent a lifetime building. At the time of his death on January 7, 1943, in New York City, Tesla's valuable papers on his invention were taken by the U.S. Government.

Life was so much similar before all these modern devices; people were nicer before cell phones and instant news. Now everyone has a platform to criticize, disrespect, or bully others. It's given us the power to take revenge on others and allow bigoted beliefs to scatter to the winds of the internet.

The controllers of our planet play the game of deceit well to make sure that you do not understand the mysteries of Earth and the Cosmos. If you did understand, our world would not be in the dire predicament it has fallen into at present.

The evidence of grand engineering and super advanced beings can be found on Earth, the Moon, and Mars, but still, they hide much from the public. Some study photographs taken by NASA prove there are structures on the Moon and Mars, yet the naysayers and the controlling powers say it's all "conspiracy theories" and you believe them. If you try to find YouTube videos and articles on such matters, you will find them disappearing before your eyes, banning such information from you because if you knew what they know, you and the rest of the world would be in control...NOT THEM!

The controllers realize that there is an awakening in the mass consciousness, and so they double down on their disinformation of information. They play the game well. For eons, they have succeeded in creating chaos to distract everyone from the truth of important achievements, sciences and the fact other intelligence are all around us.

Earth has a history of tremendous geological upheavals in response to great stress on the natural environment. Even though there is no evidence of great civilizations like Atlantis or Lemuria, they existed. Thousands of years of upheavals and water will destroy any remnants of a powerful and advanced civilization. But stories and legends live on and were handed down from generation to generation, and even ancient texts tell their stories. In days long ago, the same people who ruled in those times have reincarnated again to control our world for their self-gain. Today, there is a great war between good and evil.

We are repeating the same mistakes. Due to the Controller's

reckless disregard, arrogance, and little regard for Earth and humanity, there were huge distributions of the Earth's ecosystem. It is said that some civilizations disappeared in the blink of an eye and took many years to be destroyed by nature. People migrated throughout the world, bringing oral stories through words, poems, songs, and epic ballads of their befallen cities. They shared their wisdom, technology, and engineering skills with other civilizations. After thousands of years of inundation from the ocean has left only bits and pieces of their great cities. Many of the sky beings went underground and others beneath the oceans.

Ancient people were aware of the multidimensional share of reality and honored the spirits and the wide stratification of intelligent life. Something modern humans have forgotten. People once lived with respect for Mother Nature's order to understand her mystical technology. Mother Earth was honored as a sentient being, her conscious awareness was shared by all that transpired within and beyond her domain. Millions, even billions, of years ago, intelligent beings were observing Earth from their ships in the sky, and some in moon satellites orbiting Earth. It was understood that everything was connected *All that Is,* and Earth was honored as ONE. Most of today's religions have moved away from honoring Earth and all its life, believing that God is the whole of everything in the Universe. This caused a great chasm between the spirit of Earth and humans.

Once secret societies were created for the guardianship of important ancient knowledge. At first, these secret societies had benevolent intentions in their belief that only some would be privy to it. They know someday the knowledge would be needed again. They felt that when people healed from the severe trauma of a global catastrophe, they would be more fully capable of grasping their legacy.

Through time, the secret societies lost their way and their altruistic teachings to help humankind in future catastrophes. They became self-absorbed by their power to control the people. The Keepers of Ancient knowledge (the Templars included) became the ruling elite and used their knowledge for their own means. But exerting control from behind the scenes, they distorted the truth and lied to the people by destroying or removing the evidence of past civilizations (giants, sky people, Atlantis, Mu, etc.). In time, various secrets united in a conspiracy of silence and branched out into every country and city to exert their clandestine influence. As they grew in strength and used more deceit, they attracted dark entities who began to manipulate the Elite and their secret societies.

Six thousand years of history have been completely rewritten their way—it was edited, redefined, homogenized, and some records were even deleted. Power and control became their motto. They were consumed it the dark side of manipulation. Many Churches like the Catholic Church house volumes of secret documents never seen by what they consider "commoners".

Military organizations are an example of highly compartmentalized secret societies, and they are at the top of the pyramid game. They have hidden knowledge about extraterrestrials and life on the Moon and Mars. They know secrets about the land, sea, sky, and the universe, because their forces are always called upon to secure areas where unusual phenomena occur. Think Skinwalker Ranch in Northeastern Utah, the Bermuda Triangle, Southern Colorado, off the Southern California coast where Navy ships have encountered UFOs countless times. Their satellite technology provides the latest surveillance for activities beneath the Earth, on the Earth's surface, and in the heavens.

Creating a war has been used as a cover for entering an area to plunder and destroy, or steal records of the ancient past, and to traumatize a people into forgetfulness. Most officers and military are aware of what is going on in covert Black Op government rooms. Wiping out history is a common military procedure.

When history is destroyed, people are traumatized into another belief and emotional intelligence is suppressed, the ability to link to the high mind is shut down, and in the absence of emotional morality, countless reasons for war can be devised. The rationale for war has always been the belief that "right is might," and because most humans still carry unresolved catastrophic gene markers, they cannot remember the past and are therefore easily swayed by propaganda and mind control techniques.

Even though things appear dire at this time, take heart. With intense cosmic energies and the awakening of humanity, these layers of deception can no longer work for the Elite. They can no longer hide and cover up their dark works as the truth is revealed.

When it comes to predicting what humans will do, free will falls into place. What I foresee with leaders, countries, and politicians can be altered by human will. However, when it comes to the deaths of famous people that have already been determined from birth. I predicted in my book, *Prophecy 2022 and Beyond,* that UK's Queen Elizabeth II would not live past the year 2022. She passed on September 8, 2022, at the age of 96. I predicted that Trump would win in 2016, six months before he was elected when I was given a vision of him taking the oath of President in a long overcoat and his wife, Melania, standing by him in a light colored-coat. It happened as I had envisioned.

When I receive powerful visions like that, I know that it was destiny that he become President and not Hillary Clinton. Most psychics predicted Hillary would be the 45th President. Of course, I am not infallible. Not all my predictions come to pass, but a large number of them do. Time and space are funny things. The future is malleable, and events can be altered. Everything is connected to the skeins of time.

Prime Events drastically change the future. One example of a pre-planned Prime Event took place on September 11, 2001, when planes piloted by terrorists hit the New York City World Trade Towers and brought them down. Prime Events can be used for the good of humanity or to control humanity. A Prime Event can be for the good of humanity or another ploy to control us. For instance, the Harmonic Convergence on the weekend of August 16-17, 1987, was organized by Dr. Jose Argüelles and took place without the aid of the internet. This was the world's first synchronized global peace meditation. The event coincided with an exceptional alignment of the planets in the Solar System.

Another Prime happened on November 22, 1963, when President John F. Kennedy was assassination in Dallas, Texas. The events of September 11, 2001, created horror, anger, and profound grief around the world. Think how our world changed suddenly on those specific dates. With 9-11 more of our freedom vanished and it continues to vanish with the current leaders. The COVID-19 pandemic is another primary event that was used to bring about tyranny against humanity.

The future is penetrated from the outside—from the future. The secret societies have incredible knowledge about probabilities and how to insert themselves into the variable of electromagnetic portals. If the corridors are not traveled with knowledge, many events can blindly trample through what is called *time*, moving from one place to another like tidal waves pulverizing existence.

To establish a new timeline and a whole new web, the event that anchors time must be a profound implosion that affects all of existence. Otherwise, the web has nowhere to go. Those who own the timeline to Earth have been keeping Earth isolated, and not allowing free commerce to come and go on the timeline.

Timelines, the fabric of time, and the tubes that run on this fabric of time are all hooked into Primary Events. Without a primary event, you cannot hook into a timeline. In other words, the secondary and tertiary webs need to be hooked into a primary event, so that other timelines can use it as an anchor.

The splitting of the atom and the atomic bomb were other examples of primary events.

Unfortunately, this knowledge is in the hands of the Elite or Family of Dark, and they have misused it to control Earth and humans for eons. Some own the corridors of time or believe they do. They are reconstructing the prime corridors and organizing new eras of existence. Once these corridors are built, many forms of intelligence will be able to move back and forth, with the so-called owners of these corridors determining which forces are allowed to enter. Right now, those of lower vibrations and darker entities are entering our world like never before. UFO sightings are increasing.

Do you think it is a coincidence that huge numbers of humans are hooked on drugs in major cities and that allows lower entities to enter their bodies and enter our world? They are possessed. Every day we hear news stories about mindless drug zombies killing people on the city streets. And most criminals can't explain why they kill.

You are going to see spectacular things, but you will also see horrible things to come. You are living in incredulously dangerous times, much more dangerous than you can imagine.

Prophecy Now

CHAPTER SIX
Biden Debacle

How's Biden working out for all of you? At the beginning of 2021, I predicted in my book, *2021 Looking into the Future*, that Joe Biden would go down in history books as one of the worst United States Presidents. Sadly, for America, this prediction is becoming reality. During most of 2020, Joe Biden stayed at his Delaware home and seldom came out of his house to talk to the public, and the news media or hold rallies before the November election. There was speculation that his increasing cognitive problems, perhaps signs of dementia were hidden from the public by his handlers.

Since Biden took office, he has reversed everything that President Trump accomplished for Americans. The United States was the number one producer of oil and natural gas in the world during Trump's administration from 2016 to 2020. Gasoline was $1.61 to $2.24 a gallon in 2019, our southern borders were secure, the DOW closed 20,000 for the first in 2017 and topped 30,000 in 2020, people were marking money on their 401Ks, Middle-Class family income increased by nearly $,6000, crime was lower than in 2022, manufacturing returned from foreign countries, a typical family of four earning $75,000 received an income tax cut of more than $2,000, signed the Tax Cuts and Jobs Act—the largest tax reform package in history, and Trump was able great strides with China, Russia, North Korea, and the Mid-East. Trump made 100 megahertz of crucial mid-band spectrum available for commercial operations, a key factor in driving widespread 5G access across rural America.

The crime in our country is out of control in major cities with homelessness and from five million or more illegal migrants and cartel leaders entering the U.S. thank to Biden and his open border policy. Recently police pulled a bus over in Montgomery, New York, on suspicion of human trafficking. It turns out the bus was carrying about 50 teenagers from Guatemala, and Venezuela, migrants, mostly teenage girls. And there were only three adults on the bus. The adults were from Texas. The plane came from Texas, but nobody knows where the buses were going. The police called the Department of Homeland Security, but they had no idea what was going on, which shouldn't surprise you. And then, the police called Health and Human Services, which put out a statement that said the teenage girls were being "taken to sponsors" —whatever that means. Only three adults with the teenage girls were taken to unknown "sponsors."

And this was the third plane that had come in with underaged migrants, just in a week, to this one airport in the middle of nowhere. No one in history has flown the number of teenagers more than Joe Biden and his Administration. Not even Jeffrey Epstein. Is he reuniting all of these kids with their families? No, most of these teenagers are going to unvetted sponsors.

So, who do you think is willing to "sponsor" an underaged girl from Guatemala? How about drug cartels, sexual predators, sex traffickers, and maybe Satanists?

But Biden isn't cognitive of what is happening. Biden has lost it. He was told a week earlier that Jackie, an Indiana representative died, yet he stood at the podium and asked, "Where's Jackie? '

Neither President Biden nor Vice President Kamala Harris has visited the borders to see what is going on, but they want us to think it's perfectly normal to bus or fly thousands and thousands of illegals into major cities in the dark of night.

President Biden's failing mental state continues when he tries to shake hands with invisible people, gets lost on stage, and says untrue things such as his son, Beau Biden, died in the Iraq war. Beau Biden died of brain cancer. Then at a Washington event, Biden asked for the late Jackie Walorski to identify herself, forgetting that the Indiana Republican died in a car crash on August 3, 2022. Biden asked aloud, "Are you here? Where's Jackie? I think she was going to be here," the president said.

Joe Biden turns 80 years old on November 20, and he is the oldest president in the history of the United States to be elected president. The major news media and his defenders often brushed off his mental issues as gaffes. If you voted for Biden who has a long history of doing nothing as a senator and vice president to Barack Obama, then you didn't do your due diligence. Even Obama realized Joe is a walking disaster. He reportedly said, "Don't underestimate Joe's ability to f... things up."

Biden's record of incredulous statements includes asking Missouri state Senator Chuck Graham to stand up during a 2008 campaign event — before realizing too late that Graham was in a wheelchair. "Stand up, Chuck, let them see you," Biden said. "Oh —God loves you, what am I talking about? I tell you what, you're making everyone else stand up, though, pal."

In January of 2022, Biden told students at a historically black college in Atlanta that he was arrested during the civil rights protests in the 1960s. There's no evidence that ever happened.

In only two years, gas has increased by over two dollars a gallon and now we are hearing that Joe Biden is sending our oil and gas reserves to European countries. As of January 2022, Biden stopped oil drilling in America so now the United States is dependent on foreign oil. Diesel is predicted to run out by the end of November 2022. Biden flew to Saudi Arabia to meet with Crown Prince Mohammed bin Salman and beg for oil but was turned down. Biden once pledged to make Saudi Arabia a "pariah" (an outcast) country over its human rights record.

Biden wants Venezuelan oil, but so far nothing has been negotiated with dictator Nicolás Maduro. The Biden administration sent delegations to Caracas where the two sides negotiated a prisoner swap that freed seven Americans, including five oil executives. They also discussed easing U.S. sanctions; a move that could help U.S.-based Chevron expand its oil operations in Venezuela. Venezuela is home to the world's largest proven oil reserves and used to produce nearly 3 million barrels of oil per day. That figure dropped to just 534,000 in October, according to Reuters.

Biden has spent $3.8 trillion on his pet projects like the Infrastructure Bill and Inflation Reduction Act. Plus, he gave $1.9 trillion on the Coronavirus relief package in 2021 to citizens during COVID, and now a large percentage of people refuse to return to the workforce. Have you noticed how many businesses in your town or city are posting ads for employees? Businesses can't find help. Now the country has over 8.2 % inflation and rising as people struggle to buy groceries, gasoline, and oil for heat.

Since Biden became President, a huge amount of Fentanyl has flooded the United States through Mexican drug cartels. The Fentanyl is made in China, a country that wants to destroy America, and then shipped to Mexico where it is brought over the U.S. border. There have been 96,779 drug overdose deaths from March 2020 to March 2021. We don't even know how many homeless people have overdosed on drugs since Fentanyl hit the streets. Children are targeted by the cartel, and many believe they are getting something benign from a dealer when in fact it is the killer Fentanyl.

Despite what the major media, Biden, and Democrats say, crime has increased everywhere since 2020 and the riots in major cities. Have you noticed all the businesses being robbed during the day and night? These young black criminals don't care who they target and who they hurt. It's a free for all. No one tries to stop them. With police departments defunded across the country, and police warned not to harm anyone, their hands are tied with all the crime. Biden insists that the Democrats have a great record on crime in their cities. I guess the videos of heinous crimes are just a figment of our imaginations.

Biden is NOT running the Whitehouse or America but it appears Obama is. In fact, it appears both Obama and Bill Clinton have been running the show from the beginning. Obama use to talk about his third term, and this is the only way legally and constitutionally Obama could have ever been in the presidency for a third term. To destroy a country, you must destroy it from within.

Although a growing number of Republicans want to impeach Biden because of his involvement with his son Hunter in multimillion-dollar deals with China, they don't want V.P. Kamala Harris taking the seat of President. But Joe Biden's mental decline is fading fast, and I foresee that he will need to be removed from office by the end of 2023. I'm not clear how this will all play out with Joe Biden out of office, but we all need to pray that Kamala Harris doesn't become President. If you thought things are bad now, it would be a total train wreck with her.

CHAPTER SEVEN

Trump and DeSantis

From the beginning, I predicted Trump's presidential victory in 2016, six-plus months before he was elected. You can still find my prediction on the NewsMax website. My predictions also included that he would never be impeached. A few followers on my blog told me that Trump was impeached but that is incorrect. Congress passed to impeach him, but the Senate acquitted him twice. If he had been impeached, he'd never run for office again. I don't see anything happening to Trump regarding the joke of a January 6 Hearing. The Democrats are losing ground on the January 6 hearings that they have dubbed an insurrection compared to the World War II attack on Pearl Harbor in Hawaii by the Japanese pilots on December 7, 1941, where 2,403 lives were lost. How outrageous that certain Democrats would say that. It was another lie.

In a tweet on Oct. 24, 2021, Rep. Alexandria Ocasio-Cortez referred to the Capitol riot on Jan. 6 as "a terror attack," which she said resulted in "almost 10 dead." The truth was only 4 people died on January 6, 2021. According to The District of Columbia medical examiner, a woman was shot by a Capitol Hill policeman, and two men died of heart attacks, a woman died by accident from acute amphetamine intoxication.

When I wrote about Trump, it was obvious he was bombastic, but he was the best choice over Hillary Clinton in 2016. Hillary isn't the person you think she is and if you read the book, *Trance Formation of America,* by Cathy O'Brien, you will learn more about the evil deeds of Dick Cheney, George H.W. Bush, and Hillary Clinton.

On August 3rd, 1977, the 95th U.S. Congress opened hearings into the reported abuses concerning the CIA's TOP SECRET mind control research program code named MK-Ultra. On February 8th, 1988, a top-level MK-Ultra victim, Cathy O'Brien, was covertly rescued from her mind control enslavement by Intelligence insider Mark Phillips. *Trance Formation of America* is the first documented autobiography of a victim of government mind control. Cathy O'Brien is a healed and vocal survivor of the Central Intelligence Agency's MK-Ultra Project Monarch operation.

Cathy traced her path from child pornography and recruitment into the program to serving as a top-level intelligence agent and White House sex slave. The book is a definitive eye-witness account of government corruption that implicates some of the most prominent figures in U.S. politics.

Donald Trump, a Gemini, will announce his run in 2024 sometime in November 2022. Born on June 14, 1946, he will be 78 years old in 2024, and by 2028, he will be 82. Will he also suffer from signs of dementia later in life? He will only be able to serve four years. Although Trump has a large base of MAGA (Make America Great Again) supporters, will he still be as popular in 2024?

Trump had four years of accomplishments that most don't know about, and it wasn't touted enough while he was running against Joe Biden in 2021. Here's a reminder of what Trump accomplished while trying to fight the swamp creatures in Washington, D.C. that accused him of Russian collusion that turned out to be a lie.

Trump made the United States the number one producer of oil and natural gas in the world.

Kept our borders safer, although some migrants still crossed, but not millions like the Biden administration.

The Tax Cuts and Jobs Act expanded School Choice, allowing parents to use up to $10,000 from a 529 education savings account to cover K-12 tuition costs at the public, private, or religious school of their choice.

Launched a new pro-American lesson plan for students called *The 1776 Commission* to promote patriotic education. Prohibited the teaching of Critical Race Theory in the Federal government.

Signed into law *The Strengthening Career and Technical Education for the 21st Century Act*, which provides over 13 million students with high-quality vocational education and extends more than $1.3 billion each year to states for critical workforce development programs.

Signed the INSPIRE Act which encouraged NASA to have more women and girls participate in STEM and seek careers in aerospace.

DOJ charged more than 65 defendants collectively responsible for distributing over 45 million opioid pills. Brought kingpin designations against traffickers operating in China, India, Mexico, and more who have played a role in the epidemic in America.

Indicted major Chinese drug traffickers for distributing fentanyl in the U.S for the first time, and convinced China to enact strict regulations to control the production and sale of fentanyl.

Rebuilt the military and created the Sixth Branch, the United States Space Force. Completely rebuilt the United States military with over $2.2 trillion in defense spending, including $738 billion for 2020.

Secured three pay raises for our service members and their families, including the largest raise in a decade.

Established the Space Force, the first new branch of the United States Armed Forces since 1947.

I don't understand the thinking of Democratic voters in 2021 and why they voted for Joe Biden. He seldom came out of his Delaware home to campaign, and most people didn't even know his policies. I know of a few democratic women in Idaho who always vote democratic no matter who is running for office. They vote for Hitler if he was a Democrat. I find that shameful that they might have disliked Trump for his rhetoric and personality. Why, didn't they judge him on his merit and accomplishments instead? How idiotic to elect someone for their personality, but voters do it all the time.

Like a few politicians who have maintained the election was stolen, I also believed it wasn't a fair election in 2021. We already know that the FBI told CEO Mark Zuckerberg of Face that he had to censor anything about Joe Biden's criminal son, Hunter Biden. If the truth had been known at that time, a huge number of people would never have voted for Biden. There were also videos of people hiding boxes of ballots and removing them in the middle of the night. Who does that if it's not to defraud American voters? I just hope that the mid-term elections in 2022 are legit and that voters are safe on November 8, when they cast their votes across the country.

In 2024, Donald Trump will be returning to the first year of his nine-year cycle in numerology. One is the beginning of new experiences, new beginnings, initiative, decisions, and determination. Donald Trump will shine in 2024, but people might be leery of an aging president like Biden.

Governor Ron DeSantis

At this time, Florida Governor Ron DeSantis, a Virgo, is 44 years old and will be forty-six if he is elected as President in 2024. It appears now that he is growing in popularity and will announce his candidacy for president in the coming months. Ron was born on September 14, 1978, and that makes him Generation X. In 2024, Ron will be in the fourth year of his nine-year cycle. A number four will bring him work, order, foundations, and regeneration.

Ron DeSantis graduated with honors from Harvard Law School. While at Harvard, he earned a commission in the U.S. Navy as a JAG officer. During his active-duty service, he deployed to Iraq as an adviser to a U.S. Navy SEAL commander in support of the SEAL mission in Fallujah, Ramadi, and the rest of Al Anbar province. His military decorations include the Bronze Star Medal for Meritorious Service and the Iraq Campaign Medal.

Already Donald Trump shows that he is worried about Ron DeSantis even though he has announced his candidacy for President in 2024.

Unlike Donald Trump who made some risqué remarks about women, and was known to cheat on his wife Melania, DeSantis is known as a good husband and a father, and an excellent governor to Florida. He kept Florida's business going during the COVID pandemic and didn't force Florida citizens to take the COVID vaccine or wear masks. He even allowed his citizen to try monoclonal treatments at clinics. During the destructive hurricane Ian that hit Florida in late September 2022, he had volunteers and first responders on the scene helping victims. He stopped woke companies like Disney from pushing their agenda in Florida, and he banned CRT (critical race theory) in schools. He's a move and a shaker in politics and as some would say and he's "a straight shooter."

My vision of DeSantis is that he will grow in popularity and will run in 2024. Ron DeSantis, a Virgo, could be our next President and will remain in office for eight years. His vice president will be a woman, but I am not sure who. He will go down in history as one of the greatest presidents of our time.

Other Republicans who will run in 2024: Texas Senator Ted Cruz, Tulsi Gabbard (Independent), Nikki Haley, Senator Josh Haley, Kari Lake, Liz Cheney (is she really a Republican?), and former Vice President Mike Pence.

Democrat nominates in 2024: Biden, V.P. Kamala Harris, Stacey Abrams, Pete Buttigieg, California Governor Gavin Newsom, Alexandria Ocasio-Cortez, Illinois Governor JB Pritzker, Senator Elizabeth Warren, Michigan Governor Gretchen Witmer, Senator Joe Machin, and least we forget Senator Bernie Sanders, currently 81 years old.

My first wish is to see this plague of mankind, war, banished from the Earth. —George Washington, First President of the United States of America

CHAPTER EIGHT

World War III Armageddon

<u>Revelation 8:10-11</u>: *The third angel blew his trumpet, and a great star fell from heaven, blazing like a torch, and it fell on a third of the rivers and on the springs of water. The name of the star is Wormwood. A third of the waters became wormwood, and many people died from the water, because it had been made bitter.*

<u>Revelation 8:7</u>: *The first angel blew his trumpet, and there followed hail and fire, mixed with blood, and these were thrown upon the earth. And a third of the earth was burned up, and a third of the trees were burned up, and all green grass was burned up.* <u>Revelation 9:1-21</u>: *And the fifth angel blew his trumpet, and I saw a star fallen from heaven to earth, and he was given the key to the shaft of the bottomless pit. He opened the shaft of the bottomless pit, and from the shaft rose smoke like the smoke of a great furnace, and the sun and the air were darkened with the smoke*

from the shaft.

Scholars believe Revelations describes a nuclear explosion. Was this an event that happen eons ago, or did the prophets foresee this event in Earth's future? Nuclear fallout will cause radiation poisoning that damages the body's cells and is fatal. It is estimated that between 50% and 90% of people within a certain radius would die a horrible death from the acute effects of radiation. The food and water would be bitter (poisonous) and millions of humans and animals would die. The trees, grass, and plants would be burned beyond recognition. If nuclear war took place in all the major countries worldwide the human population would suffer extremely unpleasant deaths from burns, radiation, and starvation, and human civilization would likely collapse entirely. Survivors would try to eke out a living on a devastated, barren planet.

The ancient prophecies of Zechariah also described what could be a nuclear war. *"And this shall be the plague wherewith the LORD will smite all the people that have fought against Jerusalem; Their flesh shall consume away while they stand upon their feet, and their eyes shall consume away in their holes, and their tongue shall consume away in their mouth."* (Zechariah 14:12, AV).

The Warning from Jesus

Through the years I have written about and discussed on talk shows—one of the strangest events to have been witnessed by thousands of people near Fatima, Portugal in 1917. Three small children while tending sheep at Chousa Velha on one spring day in 1916 when they were startled by a snow-white radiance from the east. The orb turned into a handsome young man, whose body seemed to be enveloped in a brilliant light. The angel asked the children to come closer to him and said, "Do no fear. I am the Angel of Peace. Pray with me." Within moments, the angel was gone.

The radiant being appeared two more times to the children in midsummer and late fall. He told the children that Jesus was the events on earth. The next appearance was a Marian apparition that appeared on May 13, 1917. She claimed to be from heaven. She promised to return on the 13th day of each month, at the same hour (exactly at solar noon) until October. Then she said, "I will tell you who I am and what I want."

Before the Lady departed, she asked the children if they were willing to offer themselves to the service of God, accepting all suffering that might come to them and prayerfully surrendering it to God, living and praying for the conversion of mankind to spirituality. The oldest child, Lucia, agreed to the Lady's request for herself and her two cousins, Francisco and Jacinta.

Each month, the Lady revealed another miracle—sometimes a flash of light near a light oak tree and a faint buzzing sound. She revealed that Francisco and Jacinta would join her in heaven soon, but that Lucia would live many years to fulfill her destiny.

The Lady's ominous prediction came true. Francisco died of the Spanish influenza in April of 1919, and one year later, Jacinta joined her brother, dying from similar causes in February of 1920. The great pandemic killed 50 to 130 million people worldwide between 1917 to 1920, more than the Bubonic or Black Plague killed from 1347 to 1351. The greatest mortality from the Spanish flu was between the ages of 20 and 40, missing the very young and the very old, which makes it odd that Francisco died at age 11, and Jacinta died at age 10. In only two years, influenza infected a fifth of the world's population, and half of the U.S. soldiers serving in Europe's battlefields fell to influenza, not the enemy.

When the Marian apparition departed, a loud explosion was often heard, accompanied by a small-like cloud that left the top of the oak tree nearby. The smoke-like cloud then departed the eastern sky, the same direction the Lady always appeared.

Thousands of people came to experience the miracles taking place near Fatima, Portugal with the three children. Each month as promised, the Lady appeared on the 13th day of the month at solar noon. The people gathered could not see her. It was July 13, 1917, that the Lady told the children, "Continue to come on the 13th of each month. In October, I will tell you who I am and what I want of you. And I shall work a great miracle, visible to everyone, so that all may believe."

On September 13, 1917, at exactly solar noon, an estimated crowd of thirty thousand had gathered at the Cova to see the sun darken and the stars appear. Many in the crowd saw a great globe of light or orb approach silently from the eastern sky and descent to the oak treetop. At the same time what appeared to be white flowers or clusters of flower pedals drifted down from the sky and dissolved before hitting the ground. Numbers of people photographed this remarkable vision. People reported that an orb of light rose from the top of the little tree and moved toward the eastern horizon and vanished.

In the last few decades, people worldwide have reported sightings of orbs in the sky, including orbs creating crop circles in the UK.

On October 13, 1917, heavy rain poured down from the sky soaking the faithful estimated at 70,000 to 80,000 gathered at the Cova da Iria to witness the final miracle at the appointed hour— high noon. It was noted that many atheists, skeptics, and Freethinkers stood in the rain, ready to jeer should the promised miracle fail. Most of them believed the people were hypnotized by the children's adulation for the Lady and they too were experiencing a mass hallucination. The children soon arrived, but their parents feared the crowd would become violent if the miracle didn't happen. At exactly solar noon the lady appeared to the children as the crowd viewed a column of blue smoke that appeared and disappeared three times in the vicinity of the children. The children were oblivious to the phenomena and gazed at the beautiful Lady who hovered over the remains of the little oak tree, which by now had been stripped of its bark and branches for souvenirs.

Lucia stepped forward and asked, "Madam, who are you, and what do you desire?" With tenderness, the Lady replied, "I am the Lady of the Rosary. People must cease offending my Divine Son, who they have already much offended. Therefore, let the rosary be recited daily. Sincerely ask pardon for sins. The war will end soon, and the soldiers will return to their homes. Let a chapel be built here."

Then the Lady spread her hands and magnificent rays of light beamed from them toward the sun, which seemed to have lowered in the sky. Lucia cried out, "Behold! The sun!"

At that instant, the rain stopped falling and the clouds pulled apart, revealing what one witness, Dr. Jose Maria Proenca de Almeida Garrett, described as "a disc with a sharp rim and clear edge, luminous and lucent, but not painful to the eyes. The comparison of the sun with a disc of smoky silver, which I have heard even at Fatima, does not seem to be apt. It had a clearer, more active, and richer color, as changeable as the luster of a pearl. It was not round, as the moon is; it did not have the same character or the same light. It seemed to be a burnished wheel cut from the nacre of a shell." Note that the prophet Ezekiel of the Old Testament described something as extraordinary when he was visited by celestial beings or extraterrestrials.

Dr. Garrett continued, "This is not the banal comparison of cheap poetry. Thus, my eyes saw it. The phenomenon should not be confused with that of the sun shining through a slight fog...because the sun was not opaque, diffused, or veiled. In Fatima, it had light, and color, and its rim could be clearly seen!"

The crowd was mesmerized by what appeared to be the sun quivering in the sky. Then it appeared to spin on its axis like a terrible celestial pinwheel. It whirled faster and faster and from its rim fantastic streamers of light flashed across the sky and Earth, coloring the landscape and the crowd in a montage of colors — red, violet, blue, yellow, and white.

Meanwhile, the children were focused on the Lady, unaware of the events happening in the sky and around them. They watch the Lady, dressed in a radiant white garment with a blue mantle bordered by a golden threat, joined by Joseph and the infant Jesus, both wearing red and blessing the world. The vision then changed to what Lucia could only see, the Lady of Sorrows, traditionally associated with Calvary, accompanied by an adult Jesus. The Lady then faded as if a holographic image and reappeared again, but this time bearing the scapular as the Lady of Carmel.

As the sun continued to awe and dazzle the crowd for four

minutes longer, it suddenly stopped momentarily and then continued to spin and spew out a variety of colors. Twelve miles away school children sang a hymn of praise as the colors transformed their rustic village into a kaleidoscope of colors. Others present at the display were both amazed and fearful, asking God for his forgiveness.

For a second time, the 'sun' stopped spinning, and then it resumed with the multi-colored lights and spinning. Suddenly, the sun ripped away from its stationary place in the heavens and threatened to crash to Earth, causing intense heat to the terrorized crowd. Many in the crowd fell to their knees and prayed aloud for God to spare them and forgive them of their sins, convinced it was the end of the world.

Just when it appeared the sun was going to destroy the Earth, the fiery disc returned to the sky, in its normal position. When the shaken masses rose from their knees, they discovered that they were no longer soaked from the pouring rain earlier, and the ground was bone dry.

What is so extraordinary about his event is it was only witnessed within a 15-mile range, and not one astronomer at the time noted anything unusual with our sun that day. Some authors have theorized it was a giant UFO. Also, how could the sun be described as "smoky silver" with a rim and "not round like the moon?"

How was the Lady able to see into the future?

In 1927, Jesus supposedly spoke to Lucia from a tabernacle, instructing her to divulge part of the secret given to her in July of 1917, including what the Lady of Fatima had told her about five scourges that would befall humanity. The first sign given happened as the Lady predicted when she said, "When you shall see the night illuminated by an unknown light, know that it is a great sign that God is giving you that He is going to punish the world for its crimes by means of war..."

On January 25, 1938, Lucia watched the red sky from her convent cell and recognized it as the promised warning of the next war, World War II. While the new war was the first scourge, the second was to be the militant rise of communism. Lucia was told that if the world ignores the Lady's requests, every nation, without exception, will come under Communist domination. This message does not tell us to hate communism, but rather to recognize it as a scourge that comes to a world filled with materialism.

On the night of January 25, 1938, all of Europe and part of North America witnessed the most intense display of the aurora borealis (the northern lights). That night one of the largest solar flares in recorded times, probably an X-Class solar flare, was released from the sun and aimed at Earth. The sky glowed red, green, and blue over the whole of Europe. The immense arches of crimson light with shifting areas of green and blue radiated from a brilliant Auroral Crown near the zenith instead of appearing as usual in parallel lines. The show lasted over London from 6.15 p.m. until 1 a.m. People called the fire brigade believing that the glow was the reflection of some giant fire. Although there are records of such electronic displays setting fire to telegraph wires as early as 1857, there has not been a storm of such magnitude in recent times. If such an event happened today it would wipe out modern radio and electronic communications worldwide and satellites for months and maybe years.

The third and fourth scourges involved the Catholic Church: the faithful shall be persecuted and even martyred and the pope will have much to suffer--perhaps martyrdom. The fifth scourge possibly the most terrible of all, is that several entire nations will be annihilated. The prophecy might be a thermonuclear war (World War III) or natural cataclysms or both. We have reached the time of the fifth scourge.

Lucia announced the coming period of peace, but there would be no peace as the Lady predicted. Twenty-two years later, World War II was underway in 1939, which lasted until 1945. The chastisement was well on its way as the war, including the Holocaust claimed approximately 75 million souls.

While World War II was believed to be the first scourge, the second was the rise of communism. Lucia had said that if the world ignored the Lady's request, every nation, would come under

Communist domination. The third and fourth scourges it is said involved the Catholic Church and the faithful being persecuted and an unnamed pope that would suffer greatly—perhaps even martyrdom.

The fifth and final scourge was the most terrible prophecy of all where several nations would be annihilated. Is it possible that the fifth scourge was World War III, a solar event, or the use of nuclear weapons, or was it about another horrible cataclysmic Earth event from outer space?

Here is another event to ponder. On Monday, April 4, 2001, a sunspot called active region 9393 by scientists unleashed a major solar flare at 5:51 p.m. EDT. Radiation from the new flare was so intense it saturated the X-ray detectors on two spacecraft used by the U.S. government to determine the strength of the solar blasts. The blast was even larger than a 1989 solar flare that led to the collapse of a major power grid in Canada. Radiation from the new flare was so intense it saturated the X-ray detectors on two spacecraft used by the U.S. government to determine the strength of the solar blasts.

On that night I decided to listen to radio host Art Bell on Coast-to-Coast AM, broadcasting from Pahrump, Nevada. He couldn't contain himself as he described the blood-red Aurora Borealis lighting up the Northern Nevada sky. At the time, I lived in Tucson, Arizona. I rushed outside to witness a brilliant crimson-red aurora in the Northern Sky. I sensed that it was an ominous sign that something evil was going to befall humanity, and I was right!

Six months later, on September 11, terrorists in commercial planes brought down the World Trade buildings in New York City, killing 2,977 souls (this number totals 25 and 2+5 = 7, the number of Heaven and Angels).

Paranormal authors have suggested the Fatima children were communicating with extraterrestrials or time travelers who knew what the future had in store for humanity in the twenty-first century. Another mystery about the eldest child, Lucia, who later in life became Martia Lucia of Jesus and the Immaculate Heart, a sequestered Carmelite nun, is she never gave an interview during her service as a sequestered nun. Lucia was born on March 28, 1907, and died on February 13, 2005, at the age of 97. The Marian apparition always appeared on the 13th day of the month, and Lucia died on the 13th day of the month. Coincidence? I don't think so.

Prophetic Warning from a 91-year-old woman on her death bed

Recently, I received this email from a follower on my Earth New blog about one of my blogs how we are much closer to World War III and destroying the planet. Our leaders are so worried about global warming, yet they should be more worried about our capability to destroy the Earth with nuclear and thermonuclear weapons. It would be humanity's insanity to launch nukes.

From Robert: *Easter Evening April 16, 2017, in Arvada Colorado. My Polish mother-in-law, Maria Kafarska, was in hospice care for 18 months in our home. We brought her over from Warsaw in 2015 when we saw her health was rapidly failing: She survived the Uprising of Warsaw against the Nazis of WWII, Communism under the Soviet Union, and as a slave in an Austrian Labor Camp/Concentration Camp in WWII.*

She gave my wife a very strict frightening warning. NEVER return to live again in Europe because a Terrifying New War is Coming in the near future to Europe. The Russian invasion of Ukraine could very easily spread to war all over the European Continent in the coming months transforming into World War III.

I sense that Robert's Polish mother-in-law is right. Again, we have free will to change events through prayers and intentions, but it would take masses of people to come together in prayer and reverence to achieve a positive Prime Event.

People must awaken now rather than support the fraudulent intentions of all acts of war. Threats of war and the creation of enemies serve to keep the masses under control by falsely creating fearful emotions. It's not the people under dictators and tyrants that want to fight and die, it's the leaders who want more control, land, and money. Will the many or the few control the world? Will the few succeed with their desperate game plans to separate humans from each other and destroy life? War can shatter not only the mind but the soul. Each of you must understand the body-mind complex is highly programmable in a disassociated, traumatized state. In the face of traumatic events, a person's consciousness vacates his or her body and is reluctant to return. When humans are disconnected from their conscious will, they become unwitting participants in behavior-modifying manipulations. It's mind control. It breaks the spirit and resolution of a human.

We have already seen those who want to change history and destroy the past by altering books and destroying statues of previous wars. When the lessons of the past are ignored and rewritten, history repeats itself, playing out age-old dramas in different time frames.

CIA Director William Burns says it is difficult to determine if Russian President Vladimir Putin is bluffing about his threat to use nuclear weapons in Ukraine. But Burns added the U.S. has to take the warnings seriously. He was asked on CBS if he saw any signs Russia was intending to use nuclear weapons in Ukraine. He replied, "Well, we have to take very seriously his kind of threats given everything that's at stake," Burns said. "And, you know, the rhetoric that he and other senior Russian leaders have used is reckless and deeply irresponsible. We don't see any practical evidence today in the U.S. intelligence community that he's moving closer to actual use, that there's an imminent threat of using tactical nuclear weapons. But as I said, we have to take it very seriously."

Asked if Putin is bluffing, he replied: "It's very hard to say at this point. And, as I said, what we have to do is take it very seriously, watch for signs of actual preparations, and also—and this is the role of policymakers and I'm no longer a policymaker but to communicate very directly the severe consequences that would flow from any use of nuclear weapons," Burns said.

Defense Secretary Lloyd Austin has condemned Putin's annexation of four Ukrainian regions, warning that there is no one to deter him from his threats of using nuclear weapons.

Not long ago Zelensky, the leader of Ukraine, was ready to negotiate with Russia's leader Putin and not join NATO. But Biden dangled money at Zelensky, and he changed his mind. If Putin deploys the Belgorod nuclear submarine which carries Poseidon underwater drones capable of unleashing radioactive tsunamis it will obliterate enemy coastlines.

Dr. Doom's prophecy

You probably have never heard of Nouriel Roubini, a 64-year-old NYU economics professor and CEO of Roubini Macro Associates, but he is seriously reconsidering whether he wants to continue living in New York. Mostly because, well, he wants to survive. He says, "There's a scenario in which, in the next twelve months, Russia uses tactical nuclear weapons against Ukraine and then they attack NATO and we start a conventional war with Russia. The first nuclear weapon is gonna go to New York. Being in New York is not safe."

Dr. Doom, as some call him, feels that even if Manhattan manages to avoid nuclear annihilation, there's still the possibility of a natural disaster, like Hurricane Sandy that flooded New York in 2012, but "much, much worse," he told The Post. "In the next 20 years, most of downtown New York is gonna be underwater."

He first came known 16 years ago, correctly predicting the collapse of the housing market and the emergence of a worldwide recession. His new book, *Mega Threats: Ten Dangerous Trend that Imperil our Future, and How to Survive Them*, list his ominous predictions. This time, Roubini foresees global devastation everywhere, like a recession the end of 2022 that will be "long and ugly" to climate change, along with another pandemic worse than COVID's body count.

Roubini believes that World War III has already begun in Europe. The nation's coasts, he said, will soon be flooded. "Florida's gonna be underwater — all of it, not just Miami. Most of the South will be too hot to live in. You'll have drought from Colorado to California and wildfires like crazy all over the West. We'll have a great migration to the Midwest, into Canada. We'll have to take over Canada. Literally."

As in invade Canada? By military force? "I'm not joking," Roubini insisted. "The Canadians are gonna say no but they don't have the army. They have the land and the water, but no army to defend it. Unless they unify with us, everybody's gonna try and take over Canada. They need a well-armed US to protect them, so we'll become the United States of North America just out of necessity. I mean, there was a reason Trump wanted to buy Greenland."

So why, then, doesn't he just retreat to Canada now? "There's plenty of farmland across the border in Canada," he conceded. "But it's not just about growing your own food and having your own cows pasturing and your own water resources. You also need security, because everybody's gonna want to go there. And I've never used a gun in my life."

For all of Roubini's talk about a "nightmare for humanity" and not having much faith that "people will ever listen," there's at least some part of him that believes in a happy ending.

"I think young people are hearing the message," he said. "I'll be dead in 30 years, but they're the ones who really have the most to lose. Hopefully, there'll be a movement, an uprising against what's coming. It doesn't matter whether it's Republican or Democrats — these threats are much more severe than our petty partisan debates. This is about whether the human species is going to survive and thrive or we're gonna sink."

And if we sink, he said, "we sink together, and we drown together. We're all in the same boat. We can watch the boat fill with water, or we can work together to do something about it."

Will these horrible events happen?

Anything could happen at this time. We never dreamed that a virus called COVID-19 would kill millions worldwide. We never dream our governments would become so tyrannical, but they did because we allowed it. You must identify destructive negative things and then change them to positive thoughts. Mass consciousness can create miracles, but humans must be willing to come together in thought. You are here to restore peace and dignity to humanity. We can create another Hamonic Convergence again and change the disastrous road we are headed down.

The war is raging in Ukraine now, and although it appears they are winning over Russia, Putin could use nuclear weapons to take over. It is of the utmost importance that we realize the ramifications of war. It's an unnecessary act and it harms the soul and spiritual evolution. North Korea is threatening again with test missiles off the coast, and China appears to be joining forces with Russia. To have peace worldwide, the people of the world must desire peace and be willing to make the vibrations necessary to create it. Mary and Jesus warned that if humans didn't change, World War II, would take place, and it did.

Mother Earth will feel your intentions as they pass through the ley lines. Everything is about frequency and creating new energy. As energy continues to increase, and billions of people awaken from their deep comatose state, the choice must be by everyone to take a stand on the value of life.

No matter what you are told about climate change, it is due to human consciousness. Environmental indicators show that certain environmental factors have changed rapidly in the past few decades. Our thoughts mirror the physical world and create it in mass. Each of you must value yourself, Earth, and your place in the multiverse. You were born at this time to HEAL the wounds of fear, polarization, anger, and separation that has accumulated in the human gene pool over the past five hundred thousand years. Every act of kindness, thoughtfulness, and consideration enhances the course of life. Creator or victim is your choice. Which one will you choose to go forward?

CHAPTER EIGHT

The Future

What did Edgar Cayce (1877-1945), known as "the sleeping prophet," foresee in the future? Cayce did foresee New York City disappearing but did not elaborate on how. Damaging earthquakes have happen throughout the United States, including New York. The largest earthquakes were two 5.2 magnitude earthquakes in 1737 and 1884. There was damage to chimneys and plaster, broken windows, and objects tossed from shelves throughout the city.

New York state is in the middle of a tectonic plate and therefore has what are called intraplate earthquakes. When a magnitude 5 earthquake hits California, it's less devastating than a magnitude earthquake on the East Coast. That's because the geology along the East Coast is colder, older, and more brittle, according to seismologists. When a seismic wave hits, it rings through the ground like a bell, and it can be felt at a greater distance.

Washington, D.C. received a shock on August 23, 2011, when a 5.8 earthquake rattled Virginia and caused significant damage to some of the most famous landmarks in the national capital. No lives were lost, but property damage estimates ranged between $200 and $300 million, according to the U.S. Geological Survey. The earthquake was strong enough to crack the Washington Monument right through the middle.

Cayce gave thousands of readings while under a deep trance state and one of his predictions included an axis pole shift of the Earth. When asked "What great change or the beginning of what change, if any, is to take place in the Earth in the year 2000 to 2001 A.D.? Cayce answered, "When there is the shifting of the poles; or a new cycle begins." So far the Earth hasn't shifted its axis as Cayce claimed.

The Maya also predicted a new era beginning in the first years of the new millennium, when the present age of "Movement" ends on December 21, 2012, A.D. Neither Cayce nor the Mayan calendar got it right. But that's not to say it can't happen and the timeline has changed.

Astronomers believe the axis wobble (like a spinning top slowing) has been occurring for ages and causes the North Pole to point to different Pole Stars or North Stars. How often this occurs is unclear. According to leading scientific teams at major research centers, axis shifts have only occurred every few million or billion years and taken millions of years to be completed. According to other worthy sources (e.g., Encyclopedia Britannica Educational Corporation, York Films, and The Learning Channel), the wobble changes the Pole Star about every 24,000 to 26,000 years. In Hinduism, a full day and night in the Brahma equal roughly 24,000 years, a Kali-kalpa. Cayce stated that the ancient Egyptians knew of these shifts and the Great Pyramid of Giza was built to point to the Axis or Pole Star.

Edgar Cayce gave a reading that spoke of a change in the Pole Star of Earth. He explained that the Great Pyramid of Giza represented the various ages we have been going through. He said, "At the correct time accurate imaginary lines can be drawn from the *opening of the great Pyramid to the second star in the great Dipper, called Polaris or the North Star."* He must be using the word "great" as an adjective of importance because Polaris is in the Little Dipper, but it is, as Cayce said, *"the second star."* (SAO 209 is the first but is not shown in the accompanying illustration.)

The north pole of Earth's spinning axis points to a star considered the Pole Star. According to Edgar Cayce, we are about to see a change in our Pole Star, from Polaris to Vega. In Ancient Egypt, the Pole Star was Thuban. This marks a move into a new era, new age. *"This indicates it is the system toward which the soul takes its flight after having completed its sojourn through this solar system. The Dipper is gradually changing, and when this change becomes noticeable - as might be calculated from the Pyramid - there will be the beginning of the change in the races [he's speaking of root races not color races]. There will come a greater influx of souls from the Atlantean, Lemurian, La, Ur, or Da civilizations."*

Time Traveler John Titor on the Future

Time travels seem to be science fiction to most, but I believe it is possible and that there are intelligences that have used it to manipulate timelines. Some people claim they jumped into the past briefly and returned to the present day. It was more like viewing a movie than an actual event.

There are many examples of this throughout history. In 1901, two English women were visiting the Palace of Versailles in Paris. Being adventurous, the women followed an old path and suddenly found people dressed from the 19th century and speaking in a different dialect. The women decided to return and followed a man in the direction they had seen before. Suddenly they found themselves transported forward in time again and in the middle of a wedding from their present time.

Author and Psi Researcher Starfire Tor lectures on her theory of Time Shifts, Core Matrix, Co-Existing Timelines, and Unified Field Theory of Psi. She believes that a Time Shift, also known as an "Event Horizon Shift" or "Reality Shift" is defined as an alternation of our reality/space-time continuum. In other words, realities can change from one event to another and back again.

Starfire Tor claims to have had her personal experiences which she says were captured while filming a music video in Southern California. During one of the scenes, she was asked to ride her horse away from the camera and crew, and gallop over a short field and around an oak tree. The ride would take less than a minute. As soon as the director said "action" she began riding, leaving the crew behind her. After rounding the tree, she halted the horse and looked back, and to her utter amazement, no one was there. Feeling disoriented, she rode her horseback to where the main set was located and found the crew waiting. No one seemed to remember the incident except Starfire.

The following day the location photographs were delivered. Although the photographs showed Starfire on her horse and her crew, there was one glaring anomaly. On the left side of the photo was something that looked like an otherworldly portal or doorway. Starfire believes she went through a time vortex or stargate that day, and she has the photograph to prove it.

Numerous people have written and asked if I foresee another civil war in the United States. We have been in an undeclared civil war since 2020, and the protests and anger will be accelerated. The outcome of the mid-term elections on November 8, 2022, could trigger violence. Two years ago, Antifa members are conducting occult rituals in the streets of Boston, Massachusetts where one member was eating a bloody heart, symbolic of President Trump's heart! Many young people have turned against God, love, and compassion to hate, violence, and satanism. Violence and looting are commonplace among the black youth of America.

How can people be this hateful and lacking spirituality? It's called programming. The planners of this evil coup know how impressionable young minds are, and most of humanity, and they are using everything to mold the minds of Americans. After the events on January 6, 2021, where certain protestors broke into the Capitol, Democrats or the Left, have called all Trump supporters Nazis, KKK members, Isis terrorists, and white supremacists. How can 74 million people who voted for Trump be that horrible? They are not! But the Left wants you to believe that.

Such horrible images of the arson, violence, and looting in major cities across the nation were frightening, yet, Kamala Harris and Nancy Pelosi, House Speaker, did not condone such acts by BLM and Antifa. They were the terrorists, not Trump voters and supporters. Today we are seeing the 1950s McCarthyism and a frightening reminder of Hitler's Nazi Germany, and the unimaginable horror perpetrated on the Jewish people during World War II. Some Americans are mentally deranged humans. And we wonder why aliens won't contact us. We are just too violent.

This is how evil people have become. Republican Senator Rand Paul was brutally beaten by his next-door neighbor in 2019 after a gardening dispute. Rand Paul had six broken ribs and coughed up blood for a year, and eventually had part of his lung removed. A Kentucky. On October 31, 2022, Mrs. Kelly Paul, wife of Senator Rand Paul, slammed CNN anchor Kasie Hunt for saying that "might be one of my favorite stories," about him struggling to breathe and in terrible pain. People are so calloused.

Time traveler John Titor's warned us from his future that a horrible civil war took place in the United States beginning in 2011 but he also said that his timeline could be changed and what happened in his world might not happen in ours. But here we are, and it appears that the same events that happened in his parallel world are happening now.

For those who don't know the story, John Titor claimed to be from the year 2036, sixteen years in our future time while he answered questions on an internet blog in the year 2000. John spent four months answering every kind of question put to him and included photographs of his time machine and an operation manual. People began asking about the physics of time travel, why he was here, and what he thought of our society. Many dismissed the condescending and sometimes peevish answers by John, while others were angered or frightened by his tantalizing answers to many subjects and his predictions.

Prophecy Now

If John was a hoaxer, he certainly was a great actor and well-versed on a large number of subjects. I, for one, believe the story might have validity, especially in light of American physicist Hugh Everett's (November 11, 1930-July 19, 1982) many-world interpretation of quantum physics and the experiments that prove there might be many unseen levels to our existence and even parallel universes.

Titor was asked if some sort of new world government was in place by 2011. And John's response was, "On my worldline, in 2011, the United States is in the middle of a civil war that has dramatic effects on most of the Western governments."

Titor claimed that whenever he jumped into a new timeline that changed everything in the timeline. In 2020, a revolution began the day George Floyd, a black man, was killed by police on May 25, 2020. A group known as BLM (Black Lives Matter) sprang into existence. Although Black Lives Matter claim they are a social movement advocating for non-violent civil disobedience in protest against incidents of police brutality and all racially motivated violence against black people, that isn't what happened. Instead, night after night riots rages in large cities across America. Businesses both owned by both white and black owners were looted and burned. I have seen a YouTube video of a black woman claiming to be a Marxist and how "her people" plan to bring down America in any way necessary.

John said this about growing up. "In the year 2012, I was 14 years old spending most of my time living, running, and hiding in the woods and rivers of central Florida. The civil war was in its 7th year and the world war was three years away. The next time John was asked what started the civil war he answered the civil war will be started between the Democrats and Republicans.

Could a civil war in America in 2020 continue into the year 2027? With the police force defunded across much of the United States, it's a probability.

Since Obama was elected the Democrats and Republications in Congress have shown little or no bipartisanship. Many issues and bills remain in limbo even for Trump's administration. Perhaps events will unfold that will prevent a civil war at the last minute, but I don't see it that way. I see bloodshed and burning in the cities as we move closer to 2024.

John referred to our current society and seemed to see our world as beyond help when he stated, "Have you considered that your society might be better off if half of you were dead? While you sit by and watch your Constitution being torn away from you, you willfully eat poisoned food, buy manufactured products no one needs, and turn an uncaring eye away from millions of people suffering and dying all around you. Is this the 'Universal Law' you subscribe to?"

John showed more disdain for our society when he said, "Perhaps I should let you all in on a little secret. No one likes you in the future. This time is looked at as being full of lazy, self-centered, civically ignorant sheep. Perhaps you should be less concerned about me and more concerned about that!"

Ouch! Titor was right about the majority of humans on planet Earth who are out of touch with the events taking place and how our freedom disappearing daily. I am astonished by man's inhumanity to each other with evil rhetoric, hate, vindictiveness, and the lack of compassion shown on social media and woke news channels. Republicans say inflation is getting worse and at 8.2%, and Biden counters that by saying there's zero inflation. Yes, he actually said that and wants us to believe that.

After Trump went into the hospital for COVID, people were on Twitter and other social media wishing he were dead. I want to know who raised these horrible humans, and do they have a soul? Were they ever taught to "Judge not lest ye be judged," or "Do unto others as you would like them to do to you?" What these people don't realize is that there is a universal Karma, and what you put out into the Universe, will come back to you, whether positive or negative.

House Speaker Nancy Pelosi's husband Paul Pelosi, 82, was recently attacked at their San Francisco home around 2 a.m. by a homeless, drug-addicted, illegal Canadian man named David Depape, who hit Pelosi on the head with a hammer. Nancy Pelosi said, "Paul underwent brain surgery after being assaulted and struck multiple times with a hammer inside his home. He suffered a fractured skull as well as severe injuries to his hands and arms."

It was horrible what happened to Paul Pelosi, and that should have never happened. Nancy Pelosi never condoned the BLM for rioting and burning businesses in 2020, and now their stupid remarks have come back to haunt them. California is a sanctuary state and San Francisco is a sanctuary city which means it is open to all immigrants, including criminals. David Depape had a violent criminal past, and the police did not lock him up or deport him to Canada.

California's Governor Newsom recently went on television to berate Fox's host Jesse Watters. Jesse said it was a horrible act, and never made light of the crime. However, Newsom made it look as if Jesse was responsible for Depape's actions. The man was homeless and never watched television — and he lived off the street, parading around half-naked. Plus, if anyone is responsible for the crime in California, it is Governor Newsom who has made the state into a sanctuary haven for all kinds of criminals and deranged people. People say that there's so much homelessness in San Francisco, people are drugged out, and defecating on the streets. It smells like a sewer and marijuana.

Anyone can come to San Francisco and use any substance they want, including *methamphetamine, crack, heroin, or fentanyl*. People stuttering and stumbling, mindless zombies invading our world. That's what the Family of Dark wants us to be — all of us.

The future and past may be far more fluid and malleable than we think. In John's parallel universe, another Civil War occurred in the United States and World War III was a part of history, but I hate to say this is coming true. We stand even closer to World War III as our enemies count coup on us with drugs, indoctrination of our children, buying our land (China), and Russia's President Putin threatening to launch a nuclear warhead at Ukraine or the U.S. And China is putting their tentacles in every country. Communism is spreading faster than COVID spread in 2020.

Titor said that the civil war was instigated by the Democrats and the Republicans. He should have added corporations and social media.

I foresee two huge explosions taking place in a large city near a bridge sometime before the end of December 2022 and again in 2023. Also, many cities have bridges, and I sense it might involve either—London or San Francisco.

John may have given us a glimmer of hope by stating that timelines can be changed, and nothing is set in stone. *En masse* human consciousness can alter events and timelines, but are there enough human beings to create the *Butterfly in the Hurricane?* This is the idea that small causes may have megalithic effects.

CHAPTER TEN

All Lives Matter

What happened to America's black youth and all young people born between the late 1990s to 2010? They are known as Generation Z, the ones who feel entitled, hate America, hate adults, hate politicians, hate Supreme Justices, hate fossil fuel, and hate themselves. Many have turned to drugs. The majority of them have been coddled and want the easy way to education. If school lessons are too hard, they rebel against the teacher or the College professor and have them fired.

During my lifetime my friends have been an ethnic diversity — Japanese, Lebanese, Blacks, Jews, Persians, Cubans, Mexicans, Italians, East Indians, and Native Americans. Every one of them had a beautiful light within them, and wanted a brighter, more peaceful world. A large percentage of black youth (not all of them) are single-minded and want to take everything they believe is owned to them, which means looting stores, stealing money from strangers, and killing innocent children and adults. Our history is being taken from us and rewritten, and that's a travesty. Who are these angry young people (abortionists, BLM, climate protesters, and the Oath Keepers)?

On May 25, 2020, it began with a viral video of a 46-year-old African American man, George Floyd, crying "I can't breathe" while restrained under the knee of a Minneapolis police officer due to Floyd fighting back when he was arrested. The death of George Floyd set off a powder keg of anger from the black youth of America after his death by a police officer, but his death was caused only by the knee on his neck. A full autopsy report on George Floyd revealed that he was positive for SARS-CoV-2, the virus that causes COVID-19, and the 20-page report also indicated that Floyd had fentanyl and methamphetamine in his system at the time of his death, although the drugs are not listed as the cause of death. But it certainly contributed to his death.

George Floyd became a martyr, a saint to what became Black Lives Matter (BLM), but his life was anything but saintly. Floyd had been arrested on suspicion of using a counterfeit $20 bill when he put up a struggle with police officers. He served four years in prison for aggravated robbery. But his life wasn't always about crime. Floyd was the first of his siblings to go to college and attended South Florida Community College for two years on a football scholarship, and also played on the basketball team. He transferred to Texas A & M University in 1995, where he also played basketball before dropping out.

The protests and riots that have defined Portland for the past seven months grew to include so many other causes. Demonstrations varied from peaceful marches of thousands of people to vandalism sprees and violent clashes between smaller groups and law enforcement. House Speaker Nancy Pelosi and Vice President Kamala Harris did not condemn the riots, and certain congressional people encouraged the violence. Those black rioters who were arrested were released the next day. This violent event was never called an insurrection like January 6, 2020, protests by Trump supporters. Some January 6 protestors broke the law by entering the Capitol building, but none were armed. It is now known that certain Washington D.C. police waved protestors beyond barricades and encouraged protesters to enter the Capitol building.

Perhaps my generation, the "Baby Boomers, have a different view of reality, and their heroes like Mahatma Gandhi, Mother Theresa, The Dalai Lama, South African leader Nelson Mandela, Muhammad Ali, NASA's astronauts, Martin Luther King, John F. Kennedy, and women like Gloria Steinem and Malala Yousafzai, a Pakistani female education activist who was shot and survived to become the 2014 Nobel Peace Prize laureate. At seventeen, she became the world's youngest Nobel Prize laureate, and the second Pakistani and the first Pashtun to receive a Nobel Prize.

Plenty of Black women changed our world for the better. They include Shirley Chisholm, a politician and presidential candidate who fought for racial and gender equality, advocated for the poor, and was opposed to the Vietnam War. Katherine Johnson was another black hero who was profiled in the 2017 film, *Hidden Figures*, as a NASA mathematician whose trajectory calculations helped astronaut Alan Shepard become the first American in space. Her skills were crucial in calculating orbital equations which led to John Glenn's Friendship 7 mission in which he orbited the Earth three times.

Of course, there are countless Black Americans who changed our world for the better. Countless nurses and doctors of color fought to keep people alive during the height of COVID-19 and they are genuine heroes.

How can violent BLM protestors be considered helpful to the world? They aim to destroy America's history by tearing down statues and renaming anything that alludes to the Civil War while our cities are being destroyed by crime, drugs, and the homeless.

The shocking part of the BLM movement was started by several women who received $80 million in donations. That money never reached the people who needed it. Instead, one of the BLM leaders, Patrisse Cullors, purchased four homes for nearly $3 million, including one in Beverly Hills, California where she was throwing huge parties. Cullors, Alica Garza, and Melina Abdullah ripped people off who believed in them.

Candace Owens, an author, talk show host, and conservative political commentator and activist, recently produced the documentary, *The Greatest Lie Ever Told*, on the Daily Wire, about the $80 million BLM swindle and where part of the funds were donated to sex escorts, strippers, sex phone operators, peep show workers, Bosm workers, and others.

Supposedly, the BLM rioters were to be punished in follow-up investigations. Considering Multnomah County's record of declining to prosecute these cases, this seems more like an empty threat than anything else. And even in the cases that do end up getting prosecuted, those rioters have free rein to light fires and vandalize businesses in the meantime.

Portland has chosen to be the home of rioters for years now. The city will also likely set its new modern high for homicides, as it is well on pace to pass its 1987 record. Portland leaders and Oregon legislators have stood idly by as lawlessness has been encouraged by activists and agitators. The outcome has been predictable, and the same mindset can't be allowed to consume other cities or states throughout the country.

The tide for injustice is turning in America, and Americans are fed up with the rhetoric of change when neither Democrats nor Republicans are making changes.

Unfortunately, people like liberal billionaire George Soros, 92-years old, is a Hungarian-born American businessman and philanthropist. He survived the Nazi occupation of Hungary and moved to the United Kingdom in 1947. As of March 2021, he had a net worth of US $8.6 billion. He's been backing Left Democratic politicians and has backed some attorney generals in various states who support criminals and releasing them without bail. You'd think that a man who witnessed the horrors of Hitler and the Nazis on the Jewish people, would detest socialism and communism.

Conspiracy theorists believe he is a "puppet master" behind many global plots. His money can influence and change elections.

How do we rehabilitate black youth in the United States who were raised in broken homes and only know one way to survive in poor crime-ridden neighborhoods—drugs and crime? They need something creative to do instead of turning to drugs and high crime. Time after time we've watched them shoot innocent people on the street, loot and burn businesses, including black-owned businesses and kill each other. Yes, other nationalities are involved in crimes, but the majority lately have been young blacks, both male and female, robbing high-end stores, and killing and selling drugs.

Governors in Illinois, California, and New York deny violent crime has increased, but data proves it.

The bizarre part with this generation of rebels, and that includes all colors, is they don't believe there will be consequences for their horrific actions. When you kill another human, basically you will end up killing your soul. They will meet themselves in the After Life and have a life review of their actions, words, and thoughts. It may take thousands of years before they can reincarnate again. They have forgotten spiritual values and honoring all life on this planet. They have forgotten that the Bible tells us, *thou shalt not kill.*

How do we help these wasted lives—most have never finished high school? Who are the angry and hate-filled souls who were born into this timeline and what is their mission—chaos and destruction? Do they have any spiritual or religious beliefs?

If we look at history, other nationalities were discriminated against—the Jews in World War II, the Irish, the Italians, Native Americans, Australian Aborigines, Muslims, and Japanese Americans were held in internment camps in WWII, the native Hawaiians, and more. My friend Rod who is Japanese American was taken from his San Jose home as a child with his parents. Their business was shut down and there were taken to a horrible internment camp in Utah with other innocent Japanese Americans. They had little to eat and little clothing, and they suffered greatly from the cold winters for three long years. It was more like a Nazi concentration camp.

What if these young people were put in the military where they are retrained and reprogrammed and allowed higher education?

Not that I want to see anyone go to war, but there is a great war about to spread across Europe. Watch how desperate Putin behaves in the days to come and what he does. The United States is hurting with our military. Many have left because of the COVID-19 vaccine mandates.

Climate Protestors destroy priceless artwork

How does destroying priceless artwork equate to stopping fossil fuels? On October 27, 2022, a climate activist glued his head to the glass protecting Johannes Vermeer's world-famous painting "Girl with a Pearl Earring" at the Mauritshuis Museum in The Hague while a second glued his hand to the panel holding the work.

There is no instant way to cut fossil fuels from our lives. Electric cars and buses have shown that batteries can explode, and there are few charging stations in the United States and Canada. However, Europe has more than 330,000 charging stations, but that's not enough. Their uneven deployment means "travel across the EU in electric vehicles is not easy," the European Court of Auditors warned in a report last year. An electric car can go for 250 miles on one charge, but then what. What happens if the electric grid goes down? What if a hurricane hits your area, and you get stuck in bumper-to-bumper traffic?

An electric car is expensive, so how will all of California comply with Governor Newsom's order for all cars to be electric by 2035? What about diesel big rig trucks, boats, and tractors? He already banned gas lawnmowers in California. And California's ambitious climate change plans will end all gas heater sales by 2030.

In Europe, people are already cutting down trees and looking to coal for fuel. Politicians and governments around the world are bracing for potential civil unrest as many countries grapple with mounting energy costs, rising inflation, and low gas and oil supplies. Cold weather, combined with an oil and gas shortage stemming from Western sanctions on Russia for its invasion of Ukraine, threatens to upend lives and businesses. But as millions worry about this winter, it's really the winter of 2023 that people should be worried about. Part of Ukraine has no water, heat, or power.

Both in the United States and Europe Energy prices "are approaching unaffordability," with some people already "spending 50% of their disposable income on energy or higher.

Biden is sending most of the United States' oil reserves are shipped to China and Ukraine. Diesel is predicted to run out by November 25, this year. This might be an exaggeration, but the shortage is coming soon. China has been buying large amounts of oil for its reserves since the early COVID lockdowns when prices were low due to demand destruction. Biden ordered the Department of Energy to release a total of about 260 million barrels of oil stored in the SPR over the last eight months. Biden has been depleting our oil reserves for months now, sending U.S. oil reserves to Ukraine, Asia, and European countries.

In a prior chapter, I mentioned the inventor Nikola Tesla's inventions and visions of the future. Tesla's dream was to create a source of inexhaustible, clean energy that was free for everyone. He strongly opposed centralized coal-fired power stations that spewed carbon dioxide into the air that humans breathed. He believed that the Earth had "fluid electrical charges" running beneath its surface, that when interrupted by a series of electrical discharges at repeated set intervals, would generate a limitless power supply by generating immense low-frequency electrical waves. One of Tesla's most extraordinary experiments was to transmit electrical power over long distances without wires or cables, a feat that has long baffled scientists.

This visionary genius wanted to free humankind from the burdens of extracting, pumping, transporting, and burning fossil fuels—which he viewed as "sinful waste."

If the Earth holds energy that we can tap into, besides so-called fossil fuels, then why aren't we doing it? There are enough scientists who know what the Earth holds, yet they are bound by the greedy oil companies, governments, and corporations that control us.

Wind turbines are run by electricity, and as Texans learned in 2021, the wind turbines froze, and so did 246 people who froze to death because they depended on wind energy. Solar isn't dependable on a cloudy day. Besides, wind turbines kill thousands of birds each year.

Solar panels do not produce electricity when it is dark or in bad weather. So solar energy is unreliable, and plants require 100% backup by fossil fuels. Battery technology doesn't exist to store even one day of energy in the United States. Perhaps one-day extraterrestrials will teach us how to tap into their advanced technology for traveling at enormous speeds and defying gravity, and flying without wings. They don't require fossil fuels. And fossil fuels did not come from dead dinosaurs. Most of the fossil fuels we find today were formed millions of years before the first dinosaurs. Fossil fuels, however, were once alive! They were formed from prehistoric plants and animals that lived hundreds of millions of years ago.

Instead of the General Z young people protesting and destroying priceless artwork, why don't they use some critical thinking and come up with better clean energy solutions for the Earth? Where are the geniuses?

American Corporations are racists

Since the Black Lives Matter (BLM) movement, most of the major corporations have changed their ads to include mostly black actors. Most commercials on television now are 80% black orientated. It seems the major corporations in the United States have forgotten there are other races in the United States—Asian Americans, Hispanic Americans, Native Americans, Muslims, etc. The corporations aren't woke, they are racists. I have nothing against black ads, but they have forgotten that other nationalities buy their products as well. According to the 2020 Census, white Americans total 231.9 million, Hispanic Americans total 62.57 million, Black Americans total 41.6 million, Asians total 18.43 million, Muslim

Americans total 3.45 million, and Native Americans total 2.694 million. So, who has the most buying power?

I wonder how much their woke stupidity has cost them by expunging all other races in commercial ads. They are the racists, and equality means nothing to them. It will come back to bite them in the end! I suspect this is happening worldwide, and not just in the United States. Woke, socialist ideologies, and propaganda are being shoved down our throats, and with our precious children.

Prophecy Now

CHAPTER ELEVEN

Queen Elizabeth and King Charles

I predicted after Prince Philip died in April of 2021, that Queen Elizabeth II would pass away within months of his death. My book, *Prophecy 2022 and Beyond: The Butterfly in the Hurricane,* gave this prediction of Queen Elizabeth passing before the end of 2022. Queen Elizabeth died on September 8, 2022, at the age of 96.

Mario Reading, an expert on French astrologer Nostradamus, published a book in 2005 titled, ***Nostradamus: The Complete Prophecies for the Future.*** According to the 2005 book, one of Nostradamus's quatrains predicted the exact age at which the monarch would die hundreds of years later. In an interesting turn of events, the book also hinted that King Charles III will abdicate the British throne and his second son, Prince Harry, will become king.

I don't foresee King Charles III abdicating, but he will be outspoken and not reserved like his mother was during his reign from 1952 to 2022.

It can be noted that Harry and his wife, Meghan Markle, stepped down as senior working royals and moved to America in 2020. According to a report by News18, Reading wrote in his interpretation of Nostradamus, "Because they disapproved of his divorce, a man who later they considered unworthy; The People will force out the King of the islands; A Man will replace who never expected to be king."

The Nostradamus expert had claimed that the astrologer predicted the Queen's death in his 1555 book of poems, '*Les Propheties*'. Mario Reading in his book wrote that Queen Elizabeth II will die "circa 22, at the age of around 96."

Amidst news of his "prediction" about the Queen's death, the UK's Sunday Times reported that sales of Reading's book have skyrocketed since Elizabeth's death.

Several psychics have predicted Charles won't live long, but I don't foresee that. Charles is presently 73 years old, and he will live at least 10 more years if he doesn't die from an accident or assassination.

During the Queen's funeral, a woman came forward and said she was tortured in the dungeon underneath the castle by Satanists. I found it suspicious that she would come out and claim that during the Queen's funeral, and if such evil was taking place, how was she able to get away if she was in chains?

The Queen's Windsor Castle home is 900 years old, and is 484,000 square feet of space, 1,000 rooms, and has a secret tunnel that she used if she ever needed to leave without people knowing. It was built in the 11th century as a fortress. Also, there are secret underground passageways that lead from Buckingham Palace to the Houses of Parliament and Clarence House. But there is no dungeon. Some people will do anything for publicity and people believe them.

David Icke's conspiracy theories

David Icke told us in his 1998 book, *The Greatest Secret*, that shapeshifting reptilian aliens walk among us. They are here to enslave us. They are our leaders, our corporate executives, our beloved Oscar-winning actors, and Grammy-winning singers, and they're responsible for the Holocaust, the Oklahoma City bombings, and the 9/11 attacks. Although that sounds pretty far out, perhaps Icke is partly right about the evil on our planet. He further claims that the UK royal family is reptilian with crowns.

It's true that royal families kept their DNA to themselves and wanted to keep a pure line. But that didn't always work with a king marrying a sister. One thing that is fact is that many leaders from around the globe, particularly in politics, religion, and education supposedly dedicated to children, are part of a massive covert organization of pedophiles who use children for sex. This happens when parents are not aware of what their children do online. The houses of the rich are riddled with a dark secret of sex with family members, sex for ritual abuse, sex for calling in the darkness, and the dark god or goddess, where no vibration of love exists, only the vibration of seeking power. They use sex for empowerment.

What do you think sex abuser Jeffrey Epstein was doing with young girls on his private island in the Caribbean? The building that looked Egyptian was a place of satanic worship and sex with virgins. There might have been sacrifices there, and covered up.

Those who rape, murder, and harm children sexually, are devoid of love and do not realize it. Child pornography and child slavery, the slavery of men and women, have always been part of history but covered up. Now it is being pushed on young children in schools to control them.

Men dress like women now. Those in the highest positions worldwide have been put there because they are qualified by their perversions to hold power over others. Don't be fooled by their kind faces but look into their cold eyes. Their values are all askew. But the winds of change are coming. Angry protests will continue worldwide, and the energies will grow outrageous. There will be news stories that shock and astound you about our leaders. Eventually, you will awaken and discover that what is happening in one country is happening everywhere.

Let the people unite and divide the Family of Dark.

Honor those who are worth honoring. If they hide the truth, don't trust them.

And if we accept that a mother can kill even her own child, how can we tell other people not to kill one another? —Mother Teresa

CHAPTER TWELVE

Abortion and Life

The abortion debate rages on as humans play God with life. Instead of killing babies up to 9 months old, we should be asking when does the human soul first enter the physical fetus? That varies, according to spiritual books. According to regressed people on past lives and reentering a body, sometimes they jump in a month or two before birth and sometimes at the moment of birth.

According to the channeled book, *Seth Speaks,* by Jane Roberts, "The reincarnating personality is aware, therefore, when the conception for which it has been waiting takes place. And while it may or may not choose to enter at that point, it is drawn irresistibly to that time and place in space and flesh.

"On occasion, long before conception takes place, the personality who will end up as the future child will visit that environment of both parents-to-be, drawn again. Between lives, an individual may see flashes of a future existence, not necessarily of particular events, but experience the essence of a new relationship and in expectation remind himself or herself of the challenge ahead.

"The communication of the living cells is far more profound than you imagine. Until the new personality or soul enters, the fetus regards itself as part of the organism of the mother. This support is suddenly denied at birth. If the new personality has not entered earlier to any full extent, it usually does so at birth, to stabilize the new organism. It comforts the new organism, in other words. The new personality, therefore, will experience birth to varying degrees according to when it has entered this dimension. If the personality entered at conception or sometime before birth, then it has to some extent identified with the body consciousness, with the fetus.

"The newly entered soul or personality, as a consciousness, flickers, in that there is a while before stabilization takes place. When a baby, especially a young one, is sleeping, for example, the soul often simply vacates the body. But gradually the identification with the between-life situation dwindles until nearly full focus resides in the physical body.

"Those mentioned earlier who enter at the point of conception are usually highly anxious for physical existence. They will, therefore, be more fully developed and show their individual characteristics very early. They seize upon the new body and already mold it. They can choose whether to live or die.

"As a rule, now, those who do not enter your plane of existence until the point of birth are less able to be manipulators. Now there are some who resist the new experience, even though they chose it, as long as possible. They hover over the newborn form, but half reluctantly. There are many reasons for such behavior. They are not so much interested in manipulating matter as they are curious as to how ideas appear within matter. Poets and artists as a rule are more deeply appreciative of the physical values of earthly existence. Decisions as to future lives may be made not only in between-life conditions but also in dream states in any given life. You may have already decided for example, now, upon the circumstances for your next incarnation. Although in your terms your new parents may be infants now, or in your scale of time not even born. The arrangement may still be made."

According to the Edgar Cayce reading, 457-10, it says that the human soul becomes bound to the body after the baby takes its first breath. Sometimes it can be hours after. It doesn't say much about the implications of this or the ethics of abortion, but this pretty clearly says that the human soul is not bound at conception as some Christians say. This is supported by Ian Stevenson's research. Many cases related by Ian Stevenson are spaced less than 9 months apart.

We must ask if the growing fetus at only a few weeks old inside the womb is a soulless form or an intelligent soul within a fetus's body. Perhaps if women and men were careful, they would choose contraception to prevent pregnancy and abortion would never be considered. Should the entity be born to a single mother? Should it be adopted? Should there be two devoted, loving parents?
The possibilities are carefully explained to the entity. A lifetime of easy karma, comfort, and affluence may offer little opportunity for growth or challenge. A lifetime of difficult karma, however, may be just what the soul needs to balance previous experiences and proceed at an accelerated pace.

If a soul was born into poverty to a single mother and decided to work out the unfinished karma of a lifetime of selfishness, but at the last minute the birth mother decided to abort the child, a valuable karmic lesson was interrupted and must be addressed in this lifetime or another, depending on the circumstances. If a soul does not reincarnate at a specific time, it may need to wait many lifetimes to return for the next opportunity.

A soul may take a physical handicap, such as a short leg and a limp, to help work out the karma from the life as a soldier when the entity took pleasure in maiming and killing. The problem was not that the soldier killed, but because he enjoyed the suffering of others. This is not in keeping with the universal law of love and compassion. Since at the time of his death the entity had still not learned compassion or mercy.

There are many types of contraception available for both men and women. However, some women refuse to use any type of contraceptive and have multiple abortions that destroyed their bodies and damage their souls. There are certain situations where an abortion might be needed if a woman's life is in danger. Babies, although they can speak, have rights too. They are not soulless creatures inside a woman's womb.

It's unconscionable that some of these same people screaming about abortion are the ones in favor of defunding the police and releasing criminals back into the street to kill again. They approve of criminals being released, but they'd allow a nine-month-old baby to be ripped from a women's body and euthanized. They are the ones devoid of compassion, empathy, and love. This is murder! Recently, the Supreme Court ruled that each state will make its own decisions on abortions. How can any ethical doctor or woman who is spiritual, kill their fetus or a fully formed 9-month-old baby that thinks, cries, has a heartbeat, and kill it? We must remember that ALL LIFE MATTERS and must be honored.

There are certain situations where a mother's life is in danger if she had a baby full term and situations of rape where no love is involved in the act of sex.

We should consider that the soul of an aborted baby could have become the next President of the United States, a scientist, an engineer, or a great healer. It is not up to us to play God. We must learn to honor all life.

My friend Katie had a baby that had many health issues and disabilities. She could have chosen abortion, but she chose to keep her baby. With her love, patience, and physical therapy for her baby, the little girl thrived. Katie, a single mom, knew it was her karma to help that baby no matter what and she did. The last I heard her little girl was doing better but not completely healed of disabilities.

I've seen how parents of Down Syndrome children feel blessed to have them. Do we know why God gives us certain hurdles to get over in life? We don't always know what karmic lessons we need to evolve our souls. You will have a chance to know when you pass over into the Other Side and review the Cosmic computer or the

Akashic Records that records every word, thought and action ever made by all beings in the Universe.

What about adoption? My mother was adopted and there's a history of adoption in my family. She had a rough time growing up, but I have known other adoptees who are grateful for their adoptive parents. Who are we to judge what lessons another soul must experience?

It's inconceivable that President Joe Biden claims to be a Catholic but is pro-abortion like House Speaker Nancy Pelosi. Both visited Pope Francis this year and he described it as an "incoherence" that Biden, a Catholic, is in favor of legal abortion. During an interview with Univision and Televisa broadcast on July 12, 2021, Pope Francis spoke about abortion and Biden's position, after being asked about whether to admit politicians who promote legal abortion to Holy Communion. The Holy Father affirmed that there is scientific data that show that "a month after conception, the DNA of the fetus is already there, and the organs are aligned. "There is human life," he said. "Is it just to eliminate a human life? He then asked. As for the defense of abortion by the U.S. president, Pope Francis stated that he'd leave it to Biden's "conscience. "Let (Biden) talk to his pastor about that incoherence," the Pope said.

When the Supreme Justices decided to overturn Roe V. Wade, which legalized abortion throughout the United States, they turned the decision over to each state whether to ban abortion or allow it. In September 2021, Biden said he did not "agree" that life begins at conception. Biden however said that he respects those who believe life begins at the moment of conception and all. However, Christians who are protesting at abortion clinics have been arrested by the FBI and thrown into jail.

On June 29, 2022, U.S. House Speaker Nancy Pelosi met with Pope Francis and received Communion during a papal Mass in St. Peter's Basilica, witnesses said, despite her position in support of abortion rights.

Many claimed, "There's no such thing as an abortion in the ninth month!" Others asked if women could, as Trump asserted, obtain an abortion just days before a baby might be born naturally. Unfortunately, the naysayers are wrong. Third-trimester abortion is alive and well in the United States, ensuring that thousands of viable babies are killed every year. While many states have laws restricting abortion past a certain point (often 20 weeks), there are still plenty of places to kill a baby at the last minute—and abortionists willing to make it happen for the right price.

I pray that in the future women see birth as sacred and honor their bodies and the bodies of their children as a gift, and not a curse. Your spiritual evolution depends on it!

CHAPTER THIRTEEN

Putin and Nuclear War

War is hell on Earth. It shatters souls and creates chaos, fear, and deep sorrow. We are closer to World War II than ever with the growing saber-rattling of Russia and China. They are already conducting war exercises together and Russia's leader Vladimir Putin recently warned President Biden of a nuclear exchange. Putin believes in the supernatural and he believes that his birthday is special, October 7, 1952, which totals 7. He will be seventy years old on October 7, 2022, and I suspect he will do something so frightening it will alter the world. He wants this event to be his legacy in the world and sees himself as a 'Messianic Figure.'

Some commentators say it's "not just a war of politics, it is a holy war." Putin was born in Leningrad – a city that reverted its original saint's name of St Petersburg in 1991 – to an atheist father and devout Christian mother, who baptized him in secret. He grew up under the Communist regime, which "frowned upon" open displays of religion. In recent years, he has increasingly highlighted his apparent religious faith by "wearing a silver cross around his neck [and] kissing icons", wrote Deborah Netburn in the <u>Los Angeles Times</u>. In a televised stunt in 2018, when he was campaigning for re-election, Putin immersed himself in the freezing waters of a lake—an Orthodox Christian ritual to mark the Feast of the Epiphany, commemorating the baptism of Jesus in the River Jordan.

This email was sent to me recently and have sensed we are closer than ever to World War III and destroying most of the planet. Our leaders are so worried about global warming, but they should be worried about our ability to destroy the Earth with nuclear and thermonuclear weapons. It would be humanity's insanity to launch nukes. Would humans survive a nuclear war? The vast majority of the human population would suffer extremely unpleasant deaths from burns, radiation, and starvation, and human civilization would likely collapse entirely. **Survivors would eke out a living on a devastated, barren planet.**

Revelation 8:10-11: The third angel blew his trumpet, and a great star fell from heaven, blazing like a torch, and it fell on a third of the rivers and on the springs of water. The name of the star is Wormwood. A third of the waters became wormwood, and many people died from the water, because it had been made bitter. **Revelation 8:7:** The first angel blew his trumpet, and there followed hail and fire, mixed with blood, and these were thrown upon the earth. And a third of the earth was burned up, a third of the trees were burned up, and all green grass was burned up. **Revelation 9:1-21:** And the fifth angel blew his trumpet, and I saw a star fallen from heaven to earth, and he was given the key to the shaft of the bottomless pit. He opened the shaft of the bottomless pit, and from the shaft rose smoke like the smoke of a great furnace, and the sun and the air were darkened with the smoke from the shaft.

Our leaders are so worried about global warming, but they should be worried about our ability to destroy the Earth with nuclear and thermonuclear weapons. It would be humanity's insanity to launch any nukes. Would humans survive a nuclear war? The vast majority of the human population would suffer extremely unpleasant deaths from burns, radiation, and starvation, and human civilization would likely collapse entirely. Survivors would eke out a living on a devastated, barren planet.

After I experienced a UFO encounter in 1957, I began to have recurring dreams of catastrophic disasters—tsunami waves, violent winds, volcanoes erupting worldwide, and powerful earthquakes shaking the planet. I believe that we are headed toward some huge disasters in the coming two years if we don't wake up soon.

CHAPTER FOURTEEN

Satanism and Pedophiles

Father Malachi Martin, born July 23, 1921, and died July 27, 1999, was an Irish Catholic priest and controversial author. Originally ordained as a Jesuit priest, he became a Professor of Paleontology at the Vatican's Pontifical Biblical Institute, and from 1958 he served as a theological adviser to Cardinal Augustin Bea during the preparations for the Second Vatican Council. Through the years he became disillusioned by reforms in the Church and renounced his vows in 1964, moving to New York City. His 17 novels and non-fiction books were often critical of the Catholic Church. He believed the Church should have disclosed the third secret of Fatima, Portugal as the Virgin Mary had requested. Two of his books, *The Scribal Character of The Dead Sea Scrolls*, 1958, and *Hostage to the Devil*, 1976, dealt with Satanism, demonic possession, and exorcism.

Father Malachi Martin's accusations

In *The Fatima Crusader* article, Father Malachi Martin, a former Jesuit priest, a scholar, a Vatican insider, and best-selling author, said, "Anybody who is acquainted with the state of affairs in the Vatican in the last 35 years is well aware that the prince of darkness has had and still has his surrogates in the court of Saint Peter in Rome."

From 1958 until 1964, Jesuit priest Malachi Martin served in Rome where he was a close associate of the renowned Jesuit Cardinal Augustin Bea and the Pope. Released afterward from his vows of poverty and obedience at his own request (but as a priest), Father Martin moved to New York and became a best-selling writer of fiction and non-fiction. He often made references to satanic rites held in Rome in his 1990 non-fiction best-seller, *The Keys of This Blood*, in which he wrote: "Most frighteningly for [Pope] John Paul [II], he had come up against the irremovable presence of a malign strength in his own Vatican and certain bishops' chanceries. It was what knowledgeable Churchmen called the 'superforce.' Rumors, always difficult to verify, tied its installation to the beginning of Pope Paul VI's reign in 1963. Indeed, Paul had alluded somberly to 'the smoke of Satan which has entered the Sanctuary'. . . an oblique reference to an enthronement ceremony by Satanists in the Vatican. Besides, the incidence of Satanic pedophilia — rites and practices — was already documented among certain bishops and priests as widely dispersed as Turin, in Italy, and South Carolina, in the United States.

The cultic acts of Satanic pedophilia are considered by professionals to be the culmination of the Fallen Archangel's rites."

Father Martin said, "Satanism is all around us. We deny it at our peril. I could point out places only minutes from here [New York City] where black masses are being celebrated. I know of cases of human sacrifice — the sacrifice of babies. I know the people who are doing these things."

Veronica Lueken's Visions

Veronica Lueken from Bayside, New York began to have visions of the Blessed Virgin Mary (BVM) and Jesus over 25 years starting in 1985.

Veronica: "Oh! Our Lady is also pointing over with a very angry look on Her face. And I see—oh, a terrible . . . oh, it's—oh, my goodness! I know what it is; I see . . . I know they're human beings, but they're wearing black garments and slit holes in their faces.

And the BVM said: "See, My child, the worship of the prince of evil. You are shocked, My child? Do not delude yourselves that this does not exist upon your earth now, the worship of Satan. Pagans! Pagans in the House of God! Pagans roaming your nations, leaders of your nations giving themselves to Satan!" June 15, 1974.

On May 18, 1977, the Blessed Virgin Mary told Veronica, "In the Eternal City of Rome, the forces of evil have gathered. Secretly in secret societies, and openly by brazen mankind shall come forth revolution."

Conspiracy theorists believe actress Anne Heche was about to expose a Hollywood pedophile ring before she died on August 11, 2022. Was she murdered? News regarding Anne Heche's tragic death stunned the world last week. The Hollywood actress was involved in a serious car crash in Los Angeles last week. The mainstream media reported that she suffered a serious brain injury and slipped into a coma. It was quickly announced that she was not expected to survive and her family thought about organ donation as that had been her wish throughout her life. Days later doctors announced Heche had suffered brain death and on Friday the 53-year-old was declared dead under California law. The actress was kept on life support in order to keep her organs healthy during the search for potential recipients of her organs, and after recipients were found, on August 15 her life support was turned off. But that's not the whole story. Far from it.

Anne Heche was nearing completion on a new film that is too close to home for the powers that be in Hollywood — a film about child sex trafficking. She received numerous warnings telling her to stop working on the film. But she paid no heed. During her life, Anne Heche was always known for her courageousness, and she vowed to see the film through to its completion. But before we discuss the project Anne Heche was working on at the time of her death, we need to discuss the way she died. Because there are more than a few things that are off with this death. Celebrity deaths are often bizarre, but Anne Heche's death is one for the ages. First of all, let's take a look at the video played by mainstream outlets on the day of the crash.

The media announced Heche was brain dead, but inconvenient facts started leaking out. First of all, Heche was fighting for her life, attempting to get out of the body bag. Secondly, Anne Heche was talking to firefighters while she was being rescued. It hardly needs spelling out, but brain-dead people don't talk. And judging by the way the firefighters were acting, many people don't believe they were firefighters at all. Pay attention to this video. Anne Heche was covered up completely as if dead. She was carried out by firefighters to one of their vehicles, not by paramedics to an ambulance. Tragic, horrifying, and strange.

And there are so many questions that demand answers. The first two questions are legitimate inquiries. Why was she placed in a body bag while still alive? Why was she pushed down and restrained as soon as she tried to sit up? The list of celebrities with links to elite pedophilia is endless. Tragically, Anne Heche has joined their ranks. And she had one big thing in common with them. As a child, she suffered at the hands of a pedophile, and she was determined to protect children from suffering the same fate she had as a young girl.

Victims can go one of two ways. They grow up to become perpetrators themselves. Or they can reject evil. Rather than let her childhood crush her spirit, Heche vowed to use her time on Earth to make it a better place for others. That's why she was determined to finish filming, *Girl in Room 13*, the feature film that Heche hoped would help people take the red pill and wake them up to the deeply disturbing reality of elite pedophilia. Mainstream outlets are reporting the film will still be released. However, close friends of Heche have revealed she was fighting the studio to ensure they did not release a watered-down version. This is why the manner of her death is deeply suspicious. Single-car accidents appear to be one of the ways troublemakers are silenced by the elite. Just like Anne Heche, journalist Michael Hastings died in 2013 after his car suddenly sped up on a straight Los Angeles Street, swerved off the road, and crashed into a tree, killing him in the explosion.

Earlier that day Hastings had emailed his editors warning the Feds were interviewing his friends and family, before typing his fateful last words: "I'm onto a big story and need to go off the radar for a bit." Circumstances around Michael Hastings' fatal car crash in 2013 are eerily similar to the CIA's instructions on orchestrating secret assassinations by "hacking cars "according to the top-secret intelligence documents leaked by WikiLeaks. However, the mainstream media quickly dismissed the claim as a conspiracy theory. The idea that the CIA could have hacked into a car and used it as a murder weapon in the covert assassination of an enemy was too much for the establishment to entertain. The same is now happening to anyone who dares to question the bizarre death of Anne Heche. Mainstream media, fact-checkers, and Big Tech are working overtime to shut down discussions, limiting our freedom of speech. But we owe it to Anne Heche to ask if she was silenced for her views. As a successful and popular Hollywood insider with a social media following of millions of people around the world, the woman who refused to be a victim was in a unique position to red pill the masses.

Did Anne Heche get snuffed out like Princess Diana? There are similarities in the murders. Anne Heche was killed on August 11, 2022, and Princess Diana was killed on 8-31-1997, a date that totals number 11. Diana died 11 before the New York City Trade Center buildings came down on September 11, 2001. the number 11 is an Illuminati number that has shown up in several murders, including the World Trade Center buildings disaster on 9-11-1997.

There is more, and the odds of these events totaling number 11 are astronomical. In other words, it was all planned by the Illuminati.

- The date of the 9-11 attack: $9 + 1 + 1 = 11$
- Each build had **110** stories.
- After September 11th there are 111 days left to the end of the year.
- September 11th is the 254th day of the year: $2 + 5 + 4 = \textbf{11}$.
- **119** was the area code for Iraq and Iran in 2001. (911 and 119 are opposites).
- The Twin Towers stood side by side and looked like the number **11**.
- The first plane to hit the towers was **Flight 11** and it had **92** souls on board $(9 + 2 = 11)$. Flight 11 had **11** crew members.
- The State of New York is the **11th** State added to the Union.
- Afghanistan has **11** letters.
- The Pentagon has 11 letters.
- Flight 77 had 65 souls on board which totals **11**.

You are probably asking why would the Illuminati use a number like 11. Since the birth of numerology in ancient Greece, the numbers 11, 22, and 33 have been revered as the master numbers—commanding an extra-strength presence in the cosmos. Certain numbers have power and can be used in benevolent or malevolent ways.

Retired nine-year CIA agent, Malcolm Howard, has made a series of astonishing claims since being released from a hospital in New Jersey on Friday and told he has weeks to live. Mr. Howard claims he was involved in the "controlled demolition" of World Trade Center 7, the third building that was destroyed on 9/11. Mr. Howard, who worked for the CIA for 36 years as an operative, claims he was tapped by senior CIA agents to work on the project due to his engineering background, and early career in the demolition business.

Trained as a civil engineer, Mr. Howard became an explosives expert after being headhunted by the CIA in the early 1980s. Mr. Howard says has extensive experience in planting explosives in items as small as cigarette lighters and as large as *"80-floor buildings."*

The 79-year-old New Jersey native says he worked on the CIA operation they dubbed *"New Century"* between May 1997 and September 2001, during a time he says the CIA *"was still taking orders from the top."* Mr. Howard says he was part of a cell of 4 operatives tasked with ensuring the demolition was successful.

Mr. Howard says the World Trade Center 7 operation is unique among his demolitions, as it is the only demolition that *"we had to pretend wasn't a demolition job"*. He claims he had no problem going through with the deception at the time, because *"when you are a patriot, you don't question the motivation of the CIA or the White House. You assume the bigger purpose is for the greater good. They pick good, loyal people like me, and it breaks my heart to hear the shit talk."*

But even he admits that now, looking back, *"Something wasn't right. No good has come from this. This isn't the America we envisioned."*

Explaining how the building was bought down, Mr. Howard says, *"It was a classic controlled demolition with explosives. We used super-fine military-grade nano-thermite composite materials as explosives. The hard part was getting thousands of pounds of explosives, fuses, and ignition mechanisms into the building without causing too much concern. But almost every single office in the Building 7 was rented by the CIA, the Secret Service, or the military, which made it easier.*

"Mr. Howard explains that WTC 7 was *"loaded with explosives in strategic places"* in the month leading up to the day that changed the course of American history. On September 11th, while the North and South towers burned, fuses were ignited in World Trade Center 7, and nano-thermite explosions hollowed out the building, destroying the steel structure, removing the reinforcements, and allowing the office fires to tear through the rest of the building, hollowing it out like a shell.

World Trade Center 7 collapsed into its own footprint at 5:20 p.m., seven hours after the destruction of WTC 1 and 2 buildings.

Witnesses were shocked at how fast the building freefell, indicating that it encountered zero resistance on the way down.

Mr. Howard and his colleagues had done their job. *"When the building came down, it was such a rush. Everything went exactly to plan. It was so smooth. Everybody was evacuated. Nobody was hurt in WTC 7. We were celebrating. We kept watching replays of the demolition, we had the whiskey and cigars out, and then all of a sudden, the strangest thing happened. We all started to worry that it looked a bit too smooth.*

"We watched the tape again and again and again and we started to get paranoid. It looked like a controlled demolition. We thought shit, people are going to question this. And then we heard that people from the street were reporting that they heard the explosions during the afternoon.

When we were told that the BBC botched their report and announced to the world that the building collapsed 20 minutes before it actually did. At that point, we really thought the gig was up."

According to the official 9/11 report issued by the government, WTC 7 collapsed due to *"uncontrolled fires"* that were caused by debris that floated over from WTC 1 and 2, which had been hit by passenger planes. If the official narrative was true, WTC 7 would be the first tall building in the world to ever collapse due to uncontrolled fires, and the only steel skyscraper in the world to have collapsed into itself, due to *"office fires."*

Mr. Howard and his colleagues feared the public would see through the official narrative and rise up against the government, demanding to be told the truth.

"There were so many loose ends, so much evidence left behind. We thought the public would be all over it. We thought there would be a public uprising that the media couldn't ignore. They'd be funding investigations and demanding to know why they were being lied to. We thought they'd find chemical composites in the area that would prove Building 7 was blown up.

"We thought there would be a revolution. It would go all the way to the top, to President Bush. He'd be dragged out of the White House. But none of that happened. Almost nobody questioned anything. The media shot down anyone who dared question anything they were told."

Mr. Howard and his colleagues feared the public would see through the official narrative and rise up against the government, demanding to be told the truth.

"There were so many loose ends, so much evidence left behind. We thought the public would be all over it. We thought there would be a public uprising that the media couldn't ignore. They'd be funding investigations and demanding to know why they were being lied to. We thought they'd find chemical composites in the area that would prove Building 7 was blown up.

"We thought there would be a revolution. It would go all the way to the top, to President Bush. He'd be dragged out of the White House. But none of that happened. Almost nobody questioned anything. The media shot down anyone who dared question anything they were told."

Mr. Howard claims he had *"no direct knowledge"* about the destruction of the North and South Towers of the World Trade Center, explaining that *"CIA operations are very specific"* and that it is common to be working on a larger project while only understanding a small piece of the puzzle.

"Follow the money. When you want to find out who is behind something, just follow the money. Look at the trades made just before 9/11. These are the guys that knew what was coming. The sons of CIA agents, and government officials. Close relatives of the most powerful men in America. Cheney, Rumsfeld. They all got rich. It wasn't just the contracts awarded to their friends in the construction business and the wars and the kickbacks. It was insider trading."

Many countries including Britain, France, Germany, Italy, Japan, and Monaco launched insider trading investigations in the wake of the 9/11 attacks, believing that if they could prove Al-Qaeda operatives profited on the stock market then they could prove the terror organization was behind the attacks.

And all the evidence pointed to heavy insider trading around 9/11.

Italy's foreign minister, Antonio Martino, *said, "I think that there are terrorist states and organizations behind speculation on the international markets."* German central bank president, Ernst Welteke said his researchers had found *"almost irrefutable proof of insider trading."* Even CNN reported that regulators were seeing *"ever-clearer signs "that someone" manipulated financial markets ahead of the terror attack in the hope of profiting from it."*

Mr. Howard said that a serious study of who profited on the stock market from 9/11 would *"tear the heart out of the oligarchy in America. There is only one organization [CIA] that spans the entire world, and let me tell you now, it isn't and it never was al-Qaeda. There could never be a real investigation. The entire shadow government, as you call them now, is implicated."*

The 79-year-old, spending his final weeks at home and said he doesn't expect to be taken into custody following his confession because *"then they'd have to go after everyone else. They will just use the media to attack me. They are all on the payroll to suppress everything around 9/11."*

Here's another 9-11 insider who gave us the truth. Captain Eric May enlisted in the U.S. Army out of his Houston, Texas high school, where he worked in the nuclear, biological, and chemical weapons corps. He learned Latin, Greek, and Russian in his training for Army intelligence. He did a stint as a Latin, Russian and English teacher in a prep school. Returning to military intelligence, in his job as an Op Force Controller, his job was to think like the bad guys. Returning to civilian life, he became an editorial writer and ghost speechwriter for CEOs and mostly Republican politicians in the Houston area. After 9/11, he first supported the government's position. It was only after, as a journalist, he covered the bloody, three-day "Battle of Baghdad," which was completely censored from the American public, and after he talked with a 9/11 witness who was a Marine Captain, that May first questioned 9/11. Soon he realized that 9/11 was an inside job.

As a military man, Captain May took an oath to defend America and the U.S. Constitution from enemies foreign and domestic. By founding and leading Ghost Troop (named for the many unrecognized American soldiers who died at the "Battle of Baghdad"), Captain May decided to honor and fulfill that oath, by using his intelligence background and skills to foil another attempted false-flag attack on Americans.

May says it's tougher now for the government to "false-flag" us. Between half and ¾ of the American people don't believe the government story, whereas a quarter believes the government carried out the 9/11 attacks. Once people wake up, they don't go back to sleep. The May Day alert was a big breakthrough for the 9/11 Truth Movement that makes it exponentially more difficult for the government to carry out the next attack.

The media and political establishment have no choice but to continue down the false-flag path. They must carry out another attack to turn this country into a military dictatorship, as they hope to do. The recent Operation Impact involved a 3-state massive roundup of people in preparation for martial law. The next week there was a simulated concentration-camp drill in Iowa.

The internet, the alternative media, is now more powerful than CNN or Rupert Murdoch. But there is a large contingent within the 9/11 movement dedicated to creating infighting and pulling it down from within. What the government really hates is professionally led opposition. Thus, there are often serious attempts to retaliate and discourage leaders. Captain May himself mysteriously contracted a very serious disease after beginning his efforts, as did Donald Busman (the 9/11 NCO).

On October 14, 2014, Captain May died at the age of 54.

Pedophiles released in California

Recently, nutcase Los Angeles District Attorney George Gascon releases thousands of pedophiles, sex traffickers, and violent criminals under California under Prop 57. California has turned into a toilet state of depravity and lawlessness. Why would anyone move there? God help us.

Pedophiles are getting less than a year prison time after a range of horrific acts, including raping kids under 14, a DailyMail.com investigation reveals.

Analysis of a California database of sex offenders shows thousands of child molesters are being let out after just a few months, despite sentencing guidelines. Current and former sex crime prosecutors said the figures are 'terrifying' and 'shameful'. More than 7,000 sex offenders were convicted of 'lewd or lascivious acts with a child under 14 years of age' but were let out of prison the same year they were incarcerated, data from the California Megan's Law database says.

Others who committed some of the worst child sex crimes on the statute books served similarly short sentences, including 365 pedophiles convicted of continuous sexual abuse of a child who spent less than 12 months in prison, 39 cases of sodomy with a child under 16, and three cases of kidnapping a child under 14 'with intent to commit lewd or lascivious acts', according to the data.

Former Los Angeles sex crimes prosecutor Samuel Dordulian told DailyMail.com he was 'shocked' by the statistics and described them as 'frightening for society'. An analysis of a California sex offenders database shows thousands of child molesters are being let out after just a few months. Noah Thomas Holt, from Watsonville in Santa Cruz County, was convicted in 2013 of lewd acts with an under-14, child pornography possession and indecent exposure. He was released within a year of his conviction. 'Statistics clearly show that pedophiles don't get reformed. They're going to come out and they're going to commit again,' Dordulian said.

If you aren't outraged by the mind-control of our precious children in schools, colleges and on social media, you live in an alternate reality. Our children are being destroyed by evil Satanic people, and it's going to get worse if the Family of Light doesn't stop the nefarious actions by The Family of Dark. We've seen priests sexually abusing children and pedophiles are pervasive in our society.

CHAPTER FIFTEEN

The Swamp

Donald Trump called Washington, D.C. a swamp and he was right. It's full of swamp creatures that pose as politicians. Facebook founder Mark Zuckerberg admitted Thursday that his Meta platforms suppressed the Hunter Biden laptop story in the final weeks before the 2020 presidential election after a visit from the FBI, retroactively saying now "it sucks" the story wound up being verifiable.

"The background here is the FBI basically came to us—some of the folks on our team —and said, 'Hey, just so you know, you should be on high alert: We thought there was a lot of Russian propaganda in the 2016 election, we have it on notice that there's about to be some kind of dump that's similar to that, so just be vigilant," Zuckerberg told, "The Joe Rogan Experience," in a podcast interview posted Thursday.

Zuckerberg noted Twitter fully blocked the Hunter Biden laptop story, while Facebook merely suppressed it from being spread widely. "For the five or seven days when it was being determined whether it was false, the distribution on Facebook was decreased," Zuckerberg told host Joe Rogan.

Rogan pressed Zuckerberg on just how much it was dialed down and Zuckerberg said, "just a little bit less."
"Fewer people saw it than would have otherwise," Zuckerberg admitted, before upping his estimation from "a little bit less" to "but, it's meaningful. We thought, hey look, if the FBI which I still view as a legitimate institution in this country; it's very professional law enforcement — if they come to us and tell us we need to be on guard about something, then I want to take that seriously," he added.

Zuckerberg was not sure if it was specifically the Hunter Biden laptop story, but he said, "it basically fit the pattern."

Rogan asked if Zuckerberg has regrets about suppressing a story during the presidential election's final days. "Yeah, it sucks," Zuckerberg said. "It turned out after the fact, after the fact-checkers looked into it, no one was able to say it was false. "I think it sucks, though, in the same way, that probably having to go through a criminal trial but being proven innocent in the end sucks."
Still, Zuckerberg defends Facebook's suppression of the story after the FBI's visit.

"I think the process was pretty reasonable," Zuckerberg maintained, admitting it was "a hyper-political issue."

The DOJ (Department of Justice) and the FBI have proven to the American citizens they can't be trusted.

In all things of nature, there is something of the marvelous.
~Aristotle

CHAPTER SIXTEEN

Connecting to Nature

Both humans and Mother Earth are in desperate need of healing. We've become so disconnected from everything in life including each other. Life is no longer honored but taken for granted that how far we have devolved. We are being controlled by social media, mainstream media and leftist Democrats. They don't love you or America. If you and your children don't wean yourselves from cell phones, certain news and social media, our society is doomed. Go back to nature, experience the truth in nature with the plants, trees and animals. Nature will activate your seven chakras, especially the heart chakra.

Melanie Monteith, of San Diego, California, was diagnosed with multiple sclerosis at age 24 and plagued by symptoms for 14 years. Simple daily tasks became challenging. She relied on walking aids and walls to keep from falling. Eventually, she quit her job. Every day tested her survival skills. Then, in late 2017, Monteith tried grounding and it changed her life.

Grounding, also called Earthing, refers to the discovery of major health benefits from sustained contact with the Earth's natural and subtle electric charge. Recent research published in the *Journal of Inflammation, Integrative Medicine: A Clinician's Journal, Neonatology,* and *Health* indicate that grounding stabilizes physiology in many ways, drains the body of inflammation, pain, and stress, and generates greater well-being.

Grounding can be as simple as going barefoot in nature, including the backyard, for 30 to 60 minutes once or twice a day on surfaces like grass, soil, gravel, stone, and sand. If this isn't practical, special grounding mats and pads are available online for convenient indoor use while sitting or sleeping; people with compromised health often benefit from more time being grounded.

The activity restores a primordial electric connection with the Earth that has been lost with modern lifestyles. We wear shoes with insulating, synthetic soles and live and work elevated above the ground. These overlooked lifestyle factors may contribute to increasing global rates of chronic illnesses. Grounding revitalizes us, akin to charging a weak battery, because our bodies operate electrically, and our movements and thoughts are based on electrical signals. We are bioelectric beings.

Eighteen years of grounding research in a variety of indoor settings, plus grassroots feedback from around the world, clearly show that our bodies operate more effectively when grounded. We sleep better, have less pain, have more energy, and even look better. Here are some of the documented benefits.

Reduction of chronic inflammation
"Inflammation is intimately linked to most chronic and aging-related diseases," says Gaétan Chevalier, Ph.D., a visiting scholar at the University of California, San Diego, who has conducted multiple grounding studies. "Grounding seems to be nature's way to reduce inflammation."

Enhanced blood flow

Thick, sludgy blood is a common feature of diabetes and cardiovascular disorders. Several grounding studies have demonstrated a significant decrease in blood viscosity and enhanced blood flow. "Grounding represents a potent circulation booster; a simple, yet profound preventive and therapeutic strategy," says integrative cardiologist Dr. Stephen T. Sinatra, of Manchester, Connecticut, co-author of the book *Earthing: The Most Important Health Discovery Ever!*

Decreased stress

Tracy Latz, a medical doctor and integrative psychiatrist in Mooresville, North Carolina, has found, "Patients with anxiety issues, including post-traumatic stress disorder, generalized anxiety disorder, panic disorder, and depression, often benefit from grounding."

Improved vagus nerve function

The vagus nerve connects with and regulates key organs, including the lungs, heart, and intestines. In one study, doctors at the Penn State Children's Hospital, in Hershey, Pennsylvania, grounded hospitalized premature infants and documented improved vagal function that could potentially boost resilience and reduce complications. "These babies have a lot of health challenges," observes Dr. Charles Palmer, former chief of the center's division of newborn medicine. "It seems that they are more relaxed when grounded." More research is needed.

Within a few months of grounding both day and night, Monteith's disease symptoms receded dramatically. Her balance and stability improved when standing and walking. She sleeps more deeply and has more energy. An eye issue for which there is no drug subsided. She says her health continues to improve and she looks forward to living each day.

Troy Baker, a recovery consultant for special populations and chief program officer of the nonprofit Adapt Functional Movement Center, in Carlsbad, California, who has been overseeing

Monteith's exercise training schedule, has observed a reduction in the effects of multiple sclerosis since she started grounding. "Her body is more fluid, not as stiff. She moves much better, with increased energy and stamina."

For more information on grounding, visit EarthingInstitute.net.

CHAPTER SEVENTEEN

Mysterious Booms Continue

For hundreds of years, there have been reports of unidentified boom sounds heard across the United States and around the world. Sometimes accompanied by earthquakes, sometimes not, they have been heard during the New Madrid earthquakes of 1811-1812 and into 2022. They're often described as loud booms or moaning sounds coming either from the ground or the sky. Occasionally, mysterious booms are associated with cold temperatures rather than earthquakes, but there's more to them than cold temperatures. It happens in all kinds of weather and times of the year.

In 2021, there was an unusual number of boom reports, including a Darth Vader breathing-like noise in Bratislava in Slovakia. There were also reports by residents of Texas during the COVID-19 lockdowns. Reports have also come from the Ganges delta in India, the Bay of Bengal, "yan" in Shikoku, Japan, and Belgium.

On July 15, 2021, alien abductee, talk show host, and best-selling author Whitley Strieber was meditating at about 4 a.m. when two loud booms detonated in quick succession outside of his house. He assumed that they were firecrackers and thought nothing of it. But then, at 3:56 AM on July 23, the same thing happened. This time he was not in the house and his surveillance system recorded the sounds and the flash that went with them. A video expert observed that the flash appeared to come from above the house. Although he couldn't definitively identify the cause of the sounds, it later developed that numerous people in the area heard it and saw the flashes and reported this on the neighbors' neighborhood events app. Reports came from about a square mile area.

Earth Mysteries Investigator and author Linda Moulton Howe has been investigating the mysterious booms for twenty years and continues to get reports from concerned citizens.

This report comes from **Bashkortostan, Udmurtia, and Tatarstan, Russia on January 9, 2018.** A few minutes after midnight on Sunday, January 7, 2018, according to the video timestamp, an "explosion of light" with a loud boom sound was caught on security cameras at the same time that the ground shook "over thousands of miles in Russia." The geographic focus with the most intensity seemed to be in the region of Bashkortostan, Udmurtia, and Tatarstan.

On September 5, 2021, in Clarksville, Tennessee residents throughout most of Montgomery County from Sango to Old Russellville Pike to Woodlawn Drive called the 911 emergency call center to report that a loud boom shook the ground and their houses at 9:50 PM Central on Saturday night, September 4, 2021. Some reported seeing a flash of light at the same time. It's interesting that Clarksville, Tennessee is 50 miles northwest of Nashville and 14 miles southeast of the U. S. Army's Fort Campbell Depot, home of the Screaming Eagles of the 101st Airborne and the

Army's only Air Assault Division. Fort Campbell lies on the Kentucky–Tennessee border.

On **January 25, 2020, in Jackson County, Mississippi dozens** of people called media and authorities to report a mysterious, still-unexplained, very loud house-shaking "boom" that broke window glass and rattled homes in parts of South Mississippi and Alabama on Friday morning, January 24, 2020, just before 10:30 AM Eastern. No agency from Mississippi to Alabama to Florida claims responsibility for or knows the origin of, the sound, including military sonic booms. But whatever caused the huge boom, it broke out a window of the old Hancock Bank in Pascagoula, Mississippi, on the Gulf.

No meteorite coming into the Earth's atmosphere above the Gulf has been reported either, but it's always worth remembering that some 25 million meteors enter the Earth's atmosphere every day! Most burn up without booming explosions, but occasionally a meteorite can explode with a boom.

What happened in Mississippi and Alabama was *not* the Southern Strike 2020 military exercises planned for January 30 through February 15, 2020, at the Combat Readiness Training Center in Gulfport, Mississippi. That's when increased military activity exercises will include "loud or increased noise, low-flying helicopters and increased presence of aircraft."

According to the USGS, it was not an earthquake either. Their seismometers can detect the smallest of underground earthquake activity. But what they picked up below, "is not an earthquake."

On September 8, 2017, in Moranbah, Australia, on the northeast coast some 530 miles south of Cairns and 1053 miles north of Sydney, the local *Daily Mercury* news headlined, *"What the hell was that? Mysterious Moranbah explosion!"* Just before 11 PM local Australia time on September 7, 2017, numerous residents reported hearing a huge bang that shook their homes. A Queensland Police spokeswoman confirmed that police were alerted to a potential explosion around 10:49 PM local time (Sept. 7, 2017). The police conducted patrols, but there is no further information."

Again a boom was heard and a light flashed over Cairns,

Australia on October 7, 2017, at 11:15 p.m. local time. Then exactly one month later on Saturday, October 7th, 2017, northwest of Moranbah in the popular tourist city of Cairns near the Great Barrier Reef, that tropical beach town joined the long list of places on the Earth since 2011, that have experienced the sky suddenly filled with a bright flash of light, followed by a mysterious loud explosive boom.

Winston-Salem, North Carolina at 10:45 p.m. Eastern time on Saturday morning, October 7, fourteen hours behind Cairns experienced what Australians experienced earlier—inexplicable booms.

Linda Moulton how said that she had filed more than 100 reports on Earthfiles.com since 2011 about the unexplained booms and sky flashes around the world. But rarely has the mysterious boom phenomenon been reported with hours in both hemispheres.

So, what is going on? In the past few years, hundreds of reported cases of deafening booms have shaken entire cities across the globe. The noises have terrified people and their pets, and sometimes the booms sound as if they are coming from their living rooms beneath them. Other reports give more colorful descriptions of a boom as if someone fired a cannonball off a boat. Whatever the booms are they defy explanation.

The odd thing is the mysterious booms are never broadcast on national television, and only reported on network television stations in communities where the booms are heard. The sounds are heard day and night.

According to one report on March 26, 2019, a loud boom was heard across several counties in the Piedmont Triad area of North Carolina and was massive enough to register on seismographs. Yet it wasn't an earthquake, but authorities said it was. A few months before the North Carolina event, similar loud booms occurred in Maryville, Tennessee. Experts at the United States Geological Society (USGS) initially concluded that the booms were earthquakes, but later changed their minds and reported that they were caused by a nearby quarry blast, which is hogwash. Then the story changed two more times when Carl VanHoozier,

Community Relations Manager at Vulcan Materials Company, informed Knoxville's WVLT News that a quarry blast couldn't have caused the booms. Next, Robert Hatcher, Ph.D., distinguished professor of geology at the University of Tennessee, told WVLT News that the earthquake idea was nonsense. He said, "Usually a rumble, people who have been in earthquakes describe the noise as a train that comes in. It's a rumble that comes in, that the earthquake's way of coming through the earth. And so, you hear a rumble—there's not a boom or something like that."

A team from the University of North Carolina at Chapel Hill hoped to verify the noises with seismo-acoustic data taken from ESTA. They didn't find any events that coincided with earthquakes. They concluded, "Generally speaking, we believe this is an atmospheric phenomenon—we don't think it's coming from seismic activity," researcher Eli Bird told Live Science. "We're assuming it's propagating through the atmosphere rather than the ground."

The researchers, who presented their findings at the annual meeting of the American Geophysical Union on December 7, 2019, focused instead on listening to infrasound data—low-frequency sound that isn't audible to humans. They did pick up signals varying between 1 and 10 seconds long, associated with reported booms.

However, they are not any closer to an explanation for the noises, nor whether the noises are caused by the same type of events around the Earth. Many could be sonic booms from aircraft breaking the sound barrier, rather than unknown natural causes. Possible explanations for other events range from storm waves and tsunamis being amplified in a particular direction, and ignition of methane gas released from methane hydrate beds. Another possibility proposed is that bolides in the upper atmosphere and meteoroids are producing sonic booms which can be unseen until we hear the noise it creates. There's also the theory of supersonic jets, extraterrestrials entering and exiting dimensional portals worldwide, and ancient aliens living deep in underground bases and tunneling through the earth. There's also another theory that none of us want to consider—our planet is getting to shift its axis.

On October 6, 2022, late Thursday morning, a big boom shook parts of the Outer Banks, rattling windows, shaking pictures off walls, scaring family pets, and driving people to social media to see if anyone knew the source. The booms are a jarring but familiar phenomenon along the chain of barrier islands in North Carolina. They even have a name: Seneca guns. But what causes the episodes, which have been heard and felt for centuries is a long-debated mystery.

Thursday's single boom vibrated across Kitty Hawk and Kill Devil Hills around 11:30 a.m. The on-duty seismologist at the U.S. Geological Survey searched for any seismic activity in the area strong enough to cause the boom but found nothing. A spokesperson with Marine Corps said neither the Marines nor military partners were conducting training or flights in the area Thursday. A spokesperson for Oceana Naval Air Station in Virginia Beach said the same.

Staff at the Department of Defense's Harvey Point Defense Testing Activity range in nearby Perquimans County said they could not comment on training activity. Another possible theory is the boom was the result of training operations involving the USS Gerald R. Ford launched into the Atlantic Ocean on Tuesday, which is highly unlikely. A Navy spokesperson said there were no reports that the ship or any associated military equipment was active in the area.

The USGS has long researched unexplained booms heard in the Lake Seneca region of New York, as well as northeastern North Carolina, the Tidewater region of Virginia, and coastal South Carolina. The agency says the most logical explanation, learned from past earthquakes, is that weak, shallow quakes are to blame. "Sometimes the earthquakes create booming sounds even when no vibrations are felt," the USGS wrote on its website. "However, they do not seem to pose a threat to anyone."

On October 7, 2022, Linda Moulton Howe discussed the mysterious booms on her YouTube Channel. She feels a huge frequency change took place in late 2019 before the COVID-19 world pandemic. Our world changed. Something has changed with the interactions with this planet, she said.

I'm sure those of you reading this book sense the frequency change on our planet, some more than others. I felt it, and like Linda, I'm worried about our world and our future. Each of you has been assigned to become informed and bring about a frequency alteration on this planet. We are so divided that the frequency is chaotic.

CHAPTER EIGHTEEN

Holographic Technology and AI

Because we live in a frequency-controlled society, the ability of humans to create technologies could be greater. In a less controlled society that has greater outreach or travel capabilities through space and greater interchange between systems, technological advances are quite astounding. It's not that humanity doesn't have great scientists, but most of these inventions were stolen and kept by the Elite. That's what happened to Nicola Tesla's inventions that were far ahead of his time. We would possess free energy that surrounds Earth—and pollution-free energy.

Many of the amazing things outside this planet have been covered up. A whole new way of influencing and controlling thought was introduced to the planet by the film industry. Now we are learning about holographic technology, but those in space have used this technology for eons. They make holographic inserts—dramas that look real. They are inserted through portals into our reality. Since these space beings have been around for millions of years, humanity's frequencies have been controlled because it is quite easy to fool us human beings.

Holographic images have substance and it's nearly impossible to tell they aren't real. 3-D inserts are meant to be viewed in the sky and to influence large groups of people at once. Think of the Phoenix, Arizona mass UFO sighting on March 13, 1997. It might have been a holographic insert. Many, though not all, UFO sightings are holographic inserts. There have been holographic inserts of one religious figure throughout history, designed in many fashions, and projected simultaneously in many different cultures by Other Worldly beings. That is why some of Earth's religious stories are almost identical from one corner of the world to another when there was no physical contact.

The three children of Fatima, Portugal experienced a Marian apparition in 1917 on six different occasions, always on the thirteenth of the month and always at solar noon from May to October. The projections were like a movie, but one where humans could interact with the image. You can walk into them and participate in them and swear they are real. However, inserts are orchestrated events designed to influence and control the minds of humans. It's all about control!

There are advanced beings so clever they create a reality to hoodwink humans. Holographic inserts are beams of light projected onto this planet through portals. Incredible energy is required due to the process involved in merging dimensions. Technology does not exist in the third dimension, but it exists in other dimensions, and they need dimensional fusions. Why? Each dimension has a different vibratory rate at which the molecules move. These holographic inserts need places where the dimensions are already merged because they need to play through the other dimensions to enter here.

These inserts have been used on Earth to manipulate and control consciousness and to change the story of information to one of disinformation. Those who utilize this technology are not always bringing in light or information. The Lizzies have perfected this technology. They use it to shapeshift their appearance, so humans aren't frightened of their reptilian image. Much of the UFO and UAP (Unidentified Aerial Phenomena) are holographic images or inserts that appear and disappear at lightning speed.

Holographic inserts look exactly like 3-D reality. They are creations of events manufactured and inserted into our reality to look as if they are part of sequential action. They are used to control the minds of the observers, and it's very difficult to tell they are inserts. To an intuitive or sensitive person, they would sense something amiss. Some of the events will be real while others will be inserts designed to move the consciousness of humanity toward the "One World Order."

In the years ahead, we will have plenty of practice viewing holographic inserts around the planet. Humans must learn how to read energies. We must learn to trust our instincts and all our senses.

Scientists have discovered that when you look at something, that moment is already in the past. You think you are perceiving reality with your senses when in actuality, your brain has limited your perceptions of reality. When you get goosebumps on your arms, the hair on your arms stands on end, or when you get a strange feeling in your gut, or your intuition tells you something is amiss. That's what you must trust. Holographic inserts won't feel right.

If you are a dowser, you can detect these energy fields. Dowsing roads move differently in holographic inserts because their energy fields are diverse and vibrate at an incredible rate.

Right now, the Lizzies are ramping up their technologies to deceive us. That is why humanity needs to awaken to the truth of reality and the deception they play upon our species.

Portals are time machines too. You can traverse certain belts of consciousness you must find the proper portal to come back onto the planet in the precise period or corridor of time that you are looking for. This is how systems are kept locked and intact, and how they are prevented from being raided and taken over. There are portals/stargates located in South American, North America (Skinwalker Ranch, off the coast of So. California and in Southern Colorado), Asia, China, and other places around the world. The largest portal is located in the Middle East.

Many holographic inserts or dramas have been inserted through that particular portal to create chaos and hate in the mind and beliefs of the population. Beware of how the news media and governments want to affect your feeling centers when dramas happen in the Middle East. Because of the vortex, holographic inserts are easier to produce in that area. A religious figure or the arrival of extraterrestrials could take place there and it will all be a mirage created by 3-D holographic technology.

In the coming years, you will find your beliefs shattered. You will feel like a child learning Santa Claus isn't real and that your parents deceived you for years.

AI technology is going to get scary in the future. Human-looking robots will have human emotions because they will be part machine and part biological human. Science fiction has become reality, and we could see a "Terminator" type world in the future where AI turns on humanity. The 1984 movie, *The Terminator*, starring Arnold Schwarzenegger, is a look at a future world if we allow it.

Watch the YouTube video #ameca #tensorflow and how an Ameca humanoid robot interacts with a technician. Ameca reacts as things enter her 'personal space. The YouTube channel says, "This is even starting to freak us out at Engineered Arts and we are used to it!" In the video, the robot pulls back as the technician points a finger in its face, and then it grabs the hand of the technician.

Someday, creepy robot dogs and other robots will police humanity and you will feel like you are living the *Terminator* movie.

Your failure or sickness or other troubles started with unwise actions in past lives, and the effects of those causes have been brewing within, waiting for the right time to bubble over." – Paramahansa Yogananda (Born Jan. 5, 1893, and died March 7, 1953, in Los Angeles)

CHAPTER NINETEEN

Karma

What is karma? Our desires and actions in this life cause karma; they must eventually be satisfied or overcome. Think about all the people you have hurt or who have hurt you. Have you forgiven yourself or those who have hurt you? If not you, could be repeating the same pattern with the same souls in a future lifetime.

Of course, there is free will, or how we choose to respond to a situation. If someone hurts you, and you hurt them back, then they hurt you back, this cycle of karma could go on indefinitely. If you forgive them though, instead of getting angry, then you will not produce more karma with that person and that particular cycle will be ended.

Most of the people close to you throughout your life that you have known in past incarnations. Some are good relationships and others are hurtful and downright painful. If we hurt someone unintentionally or if what we desire is also the right thing, then there is a much smaller repercussion or karma. As long as we have unfulfilled desires and actions that have not yet been repaid (good or bad), we must reincarnate to neutralize them, which keeps us from merging completely with God. The difficulty is that each time we come back to balance out our previous actions, we create even more karma. Before we know it, we have lived millions of lifetimes and have a seemingly insurmountable store of karma.

How do we become free of karma? Very few people realize how many of their actions and desires are generated by past karma. They are acting out habits buried deep in their subconscious mind from many past lifetimes. The way out of this cycle is to renounce the false notion that one demonstrates freedom by giving free rein to one's desires. By attuning oneself to the infinite wisdom behind karmic law, one accepts God and His guidance from within, rather than being guided by desire. The more one lives guided from within, the greater one's control over outer events in life.

Love and forgiveness is the best Karma eraser.
Remember never hold ill will or a grudge against anyone, even your enemies, because you will meet them again in a future life and it may not be under the best of circumstances. Bless those who hurt you and forgive them and you will erase karma. This will bring back free will. If something persists in your life, it means there's a lesson that hasn't been learned from a past life. Pray and ask for forgiveness for yourself and others and watch miracles happen.

Awanyanka Ina Maka – a Sioux prayer to protect Mother Earth.

CHAPTER TWENTY

Honoring Animals

Animal life was placed on Earth to balance the Earth and for many species to be our companions and equals. During the 1990s, I was blessed to have experienced many Native American Pow Wows in the Northwest, sweat lodges, and learning from two incredible Native American spiritual leaders—Spiritual Leader of the Western Shoshone Nation, Corbin Harney (1920-2007), and Oglala Sioux ceremonial leader Ed McGaa "Eagle Man" (1937-2017).

Both Corbin and Ed spoke of honoring Mother Earth, and everything on it. Corbin said decades ago that water talked to him and said, "I'm going to look like water, but pretty soon nobody's going to use me. The Creator, or the spirit, passed this on to me to share with the people who were there at the time. Now, wherever I go, the people talk about their water being contaminated, and they can't use it."

Corbin protested against the U.S. Nuclear Testing in Southern Nevada, which was finally halted on 9/23/1992—the U.S. conducted its last nuclear test, code-named Divider, at an underground facility in Nevada. It was the last of the 1,032 nuclear tests carried out by the United States since The Trinity Test 47 years earlier.

Corbin's vision had shown him that the holes deep in Mother Earth were filling up with water. He saw the water filling up and what it was doing to our planet, inside Earth itself." Corbin had many visions through the years, but he didn't want to talk about them, because generally, nobody believes in what he was saying. "It's very hard for people to believe these things. I don't like to talk about them. I don't think anybody would really understand. But there are visions among us, not only Indian people, but white people also have visions.

"Some of us understand what a vision is, even though it's something that everybody has. All the living things on this planet of ours has a vision. Even the planet itself has a vision, and now it's beginning to warn us that something's going to become different pretty quick, if we don't do something about it. This kind of vision is given from the Earth to the people, but the people aren't paying attention to the visions."

Corbin asked me and others to come out from behind the bush and speak our truth. He knew his people didn't want to speak up. They stand behind the bush. Corbin was that way at first, but he knew how important it was to warn the people.

Corbin said, "We have to come back to the Native way of life. The Native way is to pray for everything. Our Mother Earth is very important, and we can't just misuse her and think she's going to continue. We, the people, are going to have to put our thoughts together to save our planet here. We only have One Water...One Air...One Mother Earth."

It makes me sad that Corbin and Ed, great spiritual leaders, are gone, and many others have left us.

Ed McGaa worried about the environment and how we have disrespected Mother Earth and all life on this precious planet. He worried about future generations and what they would be faced with from overpopulation and pollution. He didn't understand our great disconnect between nature, God or Great Spirit, animals, and each other. He wondered if humanity would perish by their own hand. He foresaw water shortages, crazy weather with torrential rains, drought, and wars.

Ed often said, "Wakaneechah Wichoni hey wichoni," which means in Oglala Sioux, "Live for those yet unborn" or "Live for the future generations." What will you say when someday, in the distant future when they, your progeny, enter the Spirit World and ask you, what did you do for the Planet while you were there?

Ed often told me that he lived the good life because he wanted to be with like-minded people on the Other Side. There's no doubt that Ed has found beautiful mutual souls. The day after Ed passed on August 26, 2017, he gave me a confirmation that he was there. My dog and I were walking in a nearby park, and I noticed five squawking birds in a tree. Although they reminded me of black ravens, they were brown, had a longer beak, and were slightly smaller than black ravens of Idaho. I searched the internet and finally found the raven species—known as the brown-necked ravens, they live in Africa and can be found as for as Kenya, the Arabian Peninsula, and the Greater Middle East.

The next day, I ran to the park to see if the ravens were still there, and they were, which was odd. Ed had blessed me with a message from spirit delivered by five African, brown-necked ravens. Why in the world would ravens cross the oceans to be in southern Idaho, especially when ravens are not known to migrate. As I took their picture (three of them had flown to another tree), I thanked Ed for his gift and message to me.

Corbin wrote one book, The Way it Is, and Ed wrote several books on returning to the natural way of living. My favorite Ed McGaa book is Mother Earth Spirituality.

African, Brown-Neck Ravens visiting Boise, Idaho

I have always loved and honored my pets—cats, dogs, horses, birds, and even a rabbit. Each of them had separate personalities and souls. I treated them the way I wanted to be treated—with respect and unconditional love. But some mistreat animals, killing them not for food but for the pleasure of killing. Some abuse or injure their pets and leave them to die. They are sick, sadistic people. And some people use animals in horrendous experiments—dogs and monkeys. This must stop.

Bob Luca and his wife Betty Andreasson Luca were abducted many times by the gray aliens and the ones Betty called "The Elders," more human-looking beings. Bob under hypnosis was told this by the aliens, "People on this plane as a whole are not very advanced spiritually. Technology is advancing. Spirituality, unfortunately, is not keeping pace. Man is developing many things which are harmful to him, which he does not understand. Man needs spiritual growth badly. When asked where do animals fit in, Bob replied, "Man will be very surprised to find where animals fit in. I told you all that is done is recorded, and many foolish people think the harm they've done to animals will not count. It will. All that the Creator's made is not to be taken lightly. From the most lowly to the most magnificent, much is to be learned."

Our beloved Havanese dog, Oreo, passed away January 4, 2022, near his fifteenth year of life in our arms at home with the help of a veterinarian. Ten days later, his spirit returned, and he proved it by closing our bedroom door daily, which I captured on this YouTube video.

I've always known that animals have souls and reincarnate. They evolve like all life. I believed this but having Oreo prove that he has returned in spirit was a huge surprise. Oreo was incredibly smart and perhaps more human than most humans. He learned words and always seemed to know what my husband and I were talking about. He learned quickly.

How do we know it was Oreo? Because after he passed, he often closed the door if we were gone for more than an hour. He would get upset as a physical dog if we were gone over an hour and would howl.

Since his passing, Oreo has made lights flicker and responded to questions. We recently moved and he's here in the new house, pushing the bedroom door and bathroom door partly closed, and has made our bedroom lights flicker.

Many people have asked why he returned when their dog or cat has never made any contact with them. Oreo was a Havanese breed also known as "Velcro dogs" because they pick one family member and follow them everywhere. We were with Oreo 14/7 and talked to Oreo like a human, treating him with respect and love. He was spoiled!!! But I think it's more than that. As someone suggested to me—Oreo and I have a spiritual connection.

Will Oreo reincarnate? I think all our pets do follow us through different lifetimes to comfort and guide us. Do animals evolve into humans? I believe they will eventually become human, but it might take millions of Earth years, not unless benevolent beings give them a helping hand. Ardy Sixkiller Clarke's book, *Space Age Indians,* tells the true story of two Native American girls and their two horses that were abducted by aliens. The horses returned smarter and more intuitive. In my book, *Lizzie Extraterrestrials Worldwide,* there are more stories of animals being abducted by aliens and returned much smarter.

I'm still learning much about the Other Side and have learned a lot after my sister Kathy passed in 2003 when she returned in spirit and started moving objects in our house—turning on the television set in the middle of the night, turning our radio off and on, causing our cat to freak in the hallway one evening, and causing the car alarm to go off in the garage. Days before Oreo passed several doors closed by themselves when I asked Kathy to help Oreo pass over.

Oreo knew it was his time when the veterinarian was preparing the sleep shot. He touched his nose to hers as if to say, "I know it's time to go." Animals are intuitive and amazing creatures. Read more about Oreo and animals that have reincarnated in my book, *Signals from Heaven*, on Amazon.

If you see an animal being abused, PLEASE take the time to call the authorities. In many states, it's punishable by law to maliciously harm any animal.

What I've learned is, "Love transcends time and space." It's the greatest energy in the entire Universe. Your beloved pets will accompany you on many soul journeys, and they will be back on future adventures to comfort you and love you unconditionally. I guarantee it!

CHAPTER TWENTY-ONE

More Prophecies

If you thought 2008 was bad with all the home foreclosures and bankruptcies, just wait until we get into 2023. Weather will be extreme this year--flash floods, extreme heat, tornadoes, straight-line winds, and hurricanes. Some places around the world will break records with heat and other places will experience an unusually cool summer.

1. We stand on a precipice of destroying the Earth and live with nuclear weapons like past civilizations. As I wrote in *Prophecy 2022 and Beyond,* we are the Atlanteans returned to fight a spiritual war against the Family of Dark. Throughout the cosmos, great civilizations have vanished either by

natural events or by warring ETs. If we fail to restore the planetary Peace and Cosmic Order on our home planet, the soul evolution will be aborted, and global destruction and mass extinction will take place as it happened in the days of Atlantis. We still have a choice to save our planet and ourselves. We think that we are protected, and we are to an extent, but we could become one more on a long list of extinct species that have either destroyed themselves or their planet if we don't awaken NOW. This has all been planned for eons in time by the Family of Dark. How has it been allowed to happen? The free will aspect is what has been exploited as the basis for their ability to manipulate humanity to be the vehicle of their power. Humans are malleable enough to be influenced into buying their agenda. This has caused a downward spiral into heavier energy rather than the lifting of vibration as was intended. However, there is a point at which their restrictive pressure of controlling the thought processes of the mass consciousness of the planet can backfire and cause exactly the opposite of what they have planned. This will cause them to miss the opportunity for the final dimensional vibratory change needed for the completion of their plans.

2. **Donald Trump** - Again the DOJ (Dept. of Justice) wants to indict Trump, but it won't happen. He will run in 2024. Although 2024 is still 2 years away, I am sensing more and more that Trump will run again and announce that in after the November 8th midterm elections, around the middle of November 2022. His numerological number will be a number 1 year. It could be Deja vu with Hillary running against him. Of course, much can happen between now and then. We need a leader who can restore our borders, recover oil and gas, restore our military and police, reduce crime, a deport millions of illegal immigrants. As the Democratic Left continues to take him to court for anything they can dig up, Trump will remain unscathed. Unfortunately, Trump will be 78 years old, and will only have four years to make

a difference and unwind everything Biden and his administration have done to hurt America. We need someone who will be in office for eight years, not four to make a huge difference. I see Florida's Governor Ron DeSantis running in 2024, and probably winning. He will make a great president as I wrote earlier in the book. DeSantis will win the Governor election in Florida, but the counting could be disrupted by a tropical storm headed to Florida. This could cause fraud in the election. Trump will be plagued by the Democrats trying to indict him or accuse him falsely of the January 6 attacks.

3. **Nikki Haley and Mike Pence will run as Republican Nominees, but I don't see them as presidential nominees in 2024. I foresee Texas Governor Greg Abbott and Florida Ron DeSantis will be re-elected in Nov. 2022. In Arizona, I foresee Kari Lake winning the Governor position.** Democratic nominee for Governor Beto O'Rouke doesn't think there is a problem with the border and will lose the election in 2022. Beto said this in a June 2022 interview: the "border is pretty great right now." Migrants are paying the cartel thousands of dollars and if they don't get what they want they kill or maim migrants and rape women trying to cross the border. Millions have crossed into the United States illegally and flown or bussed to major cities. It's a major disaster for America.

4. **GAS prices dropped slightly in July** but are rising again because President Biden is depleting our gas reserves by exporting them to Europe. Gas prices will continue to rise during the holidays and into 2023 and could reach $5.00/gallon or more and diesel could go over $6.00. Truckers will be hurt, and the high gas prices will cause major shortages in 2023.

5. **Huge shortages.** Stock up on food supplies!!! I've been predicting this for a long time. Already gas has reached over $7.00/gal. in some areas of California.

6. **The stock market will fall lower after the mid-term**

elections as inflation goes up and up. It's already at 8.2%, but Biden insists we have zero inflation. Interest rates will continue to rise and could reach 9 or 10% by 2023. People won't be able to buy homes, and many will lose their homes with inflation that turns into a recession.

7. **Water, and not a drop to drink!** Water will become the most precious commodity shortly and its scarcity will trigger riots, wars, mass immigration, and famines. Be ready!

8. **Crime will continue to escalate, and homelessness will prevail in major cities.** Fentanyl drugs will kill thousands.

9. **Recession coming:** The U.S. Fed have already increased the Interest Rate and they will do it 6 more times in 2022. Spiraling interest rates!

10. **Putin hasn't slowed his advance on Ukraine.** War III could still be looming in late 2022 with the use of nuclear weapons by Russia. Former President Obama purchased a 2,500-gallon propane tank for his Martha Vineyards estate — why? He must be anticipating a major shortage. The continued War in Ukraine is hurting the people, not Zelensky, the leader of Ukraine. I don't see Putin stopping anytime soon.

11. **The humanitarian crisis** will unfold throughout Europe as people become nomads. Homelessness will grow larger in U.S. cities. Most are addicted to drugs. Who will feed them? Canada's Prime Minister Trudeau is allowing dangerous drugs to be purchased in British Columbia and soon all of Canada. He is also taking away the guns from the population.

12. **The Weather in 2023** will be on steroids! Extreme heat, drought conditions, flooding, and wildfires again. Some areas will experience flooding and others drought. It will be a topsy-turvey world. Tornadoes will rage across the U.S. South and Midwest in late fall 2022 and early 2023. The weather will be extreme this winter of 2022-2023 and snowmageddon in Europe with deadly avalanches. The Northwest of the United States will have plenty of snow and rain in Texas and Florida. The Southwest will not see the

needed rain, but Texas will. Huge rainstorms and cold for most of the United States. A major heatwave in Australia. Many will have little or no heat across Europe and Ukraine. I foresee more hurricanes forming in both the Atlantic and Pacific in the late fall of 2023. Watch out for Florida and the Caribbean!

13. **People leaving us in 2023.** I see a gray aura around singers Celine Dion, Tony Bennett, 95. and country singer Willie Nelson, 88. Pope Francis and the Dali Lama could have severe health issues in 2023.

14. **John Fetterman, running for Senator in Pennsylvania** against Dr. Oz probably will win by a small percentage, but he will not stay in office. His aura is gray and his health is waning which is why he won't release his medical records. There's a huge bulge on the right side of his neck that is most likely a tumor that can't be removed. That's why he wears hoodies to cover it up. If it was a goiter, that would be on the front of his neck, not the back right side of his neck. He is not a well man and could experience another stroke or heart attack that will stop him from running. Does anyone understand why Fetterman was allowed to run for office when he has a hard time understanding anyone? His agenda is alarming. He wants to release criminals from prison. Opry Winfrey recently endorsed him, and she's never met him. But she called Dr. Oz "her boy" and had helped him rise in prominence, and now she's turned her back on him. Fetterman had a blood clot to his heart and didn't take medicine for it for five years. Sadly, he is a walking time bomb for a major stroke or heart attack.

15. **Watch the skies as ETs** make themselves known to us in 2022. Huge events coming. The ETs worry about our nuclear capabilities and are watching the Russians, China, and the United States' military operations.

16. **COVID and their plan to lock us down again. Already part of Southern California are wearing masks again.** As I predicted, COVID is waning this year and most restrictions

removed. Covid will always be with us but more like the yearly flu. However, thousands of people still die from the flu each year. Again, as mid-term elections grow near, we could see the CDC, Biden Administration, and Dr. Fauci will put fear into us with the new BA-5 variant. If voters can't get to the polls, watch how voter fraud takes place. They are taking their agenda from China's lockdown. How will people get to the polls if they can't afford gas for their cars? Mail in ballots--a way to cheat again for the Democrats.

17. **NASA. the Moon and Mars:** NASA's Artemis flight has been canceled twice and they keep rescheduling the unmanned flight to the moon. It's now set for November 14, 2022, but there will be more problems. How could we send a man to the moon in 1969, but we can't send an unmanned flight around the moon now? Are aliens stopping NASA from returning? **Elon Musk has hinted about a mission to Mars with a crew in 2029. It will happen, but there will be unforeseen problems.**

18. **The world's largest active volcano, Mauna Loa**, in Hawaii will erupt in 2023. It's already sending signals that it may erupt.

19. **More trouble for Pelosi:** House Speaker Nancy Pelosi will step down in 2023 to Republican Kevin McCarthy. More problems for Nancy's husband Paul after a DUI car accident and his skull fractured by an illegal Canadian homeless man. Eventually, the video will be released of the incident, which appears to have many holes.

20. **Earth changes** -Earth will shake as it has never shaken, and volcanoes will erupt that have been dormant for years. Tsunamis will happen especially in the South Pacific and Asian countries. A massive deluge of water worldwide. This will be the norm in the coming months -- extreme temperatures, flash floods, dangerous wildfires already happening, earthquakes, and volcanoes erupting worldwide. A number of my predictions in *Prophecy 2022*

and Beyond have come true on deaths, volcano and earthquake predictions, wildfires, and political and COVID vaccine predictions.

21. **World War III** - Biden and his administration has been suggesting war with Russia and Putin. We are minutes away for World War III, as Putin plans to invade more European countries. Putin is now in league with China, and I foresee China invading Taiwan. North Korea could attack South Korea. The problem is that most nations and the U.S. are afraid to do anything to stop Putin that might trigger a nuclear conflict. However, I see the release of deadly viruses. This could lead to another global pandemic. This is the audacious agenda the Family of Dark has planned for years. Be prepared.

22. **Shortages from Biden's inflation and famine:** This was planned long ago to bring down America. Watch how shortages continue—no chicken or turkeys, wheat and potatoes unavailable. Diesel running out and truckers are unable to make deliveries nationwide. This will happen in Europe, England, and other countries. Gas prices will continue to rise as well as all consumer goods. A trucker had to fill up his tank and it was over $1,000 to fill. This is just the beginning of massive shortages and it's not due to Russia. It's Biden's fault. If we started production of oil in the U.S. and Alaska, petroleum prices would go down, but that won't happen. Be prepared for the shortages.

23. **Refugees and migrants on the move:** Masses of people will be displaced this year. Starvation, food shortages, no place to live, tired of certain Marxist ideologies in some U.S. states, and high crime in cities. A human catastrophe. The Four Horsemen of the Apocalypse are riding. four horsemen of the apocalypse, in Christianity, the four horsemen, according to the book of Revelation (6:1–8), appear with the opening of the first four of the seven seals that bring forth the cataclysm of the apocalypse. The first horseman, a conqueror with a bow and crown, rides a white

horse, which scholars sometimes interpret to symbolize Christ or the Antichrist; the second horseman is given a great sword and rides a red horse, symbolizing war and bloodshed; the third carries a balance scale, rides a black horse, and symbolizes famine; and the fourth horseman rides a pale horse and is identified as Death.

24. **Nuclear warhead in Europe.** I continue to have visions of a massive explosion but I'm not sure where. This is the start of World War III. Your prayers are needed to stop this nightmare scenario. Three giants unite against the Dragon (China and Russia) - Nostradamus predicted this.

25. **Something is going to happen.** The 2022 United States elections will be held on Tuesday, November 8, 2022. During this midterm election year, all 435 seats in the House of Representatives and 35 of the 100 seats in the Senate will be contested.

26. **President Joe Biden** - Biden will go down in history as the worst President and Kamala Harris as the worst V.P. in history. His dementia will worsen as time goes on. Biden's term may come to an abrupt end before the end of 2023. He could be removed because of dementia, but don't rule out impeachment when more is uncovered about the Biden crime family and his illegal involvement with his son Hunter Biden. Joe Biden's odds of winning a potential re-election bid are waning: the president's approval rating is dropping and even his own party doesn't want him to run in 2024.

27. **Social media**--Twitter, and Facebook are going down because of their cancel culture forced on everyone! If you are on the LEFT, you can post anything, but if you say anything against the LEFT, you are canceled. Let's hope Elon Musk does some major housecleaning at Twitter.

28. **Massive Water Shortages** - as the Southwest of the United States continues to be in a drought situation that worsens each year. Now Lake Mead has dropped to record levels. Lake Mead and Lake Powell upstream are the largest

human-made reservoirs in the U.S., part of a system that provides water to more than 40 million people, tribes, agriculture, and industry in Arizona, California, Colorado, Nevada, New Mexico, Utah, Wyoming and across the southern border in Mexico. The problem is authorities should be conserving water, but they aren't. I suggest that if you live in these areas to relocate the Northern States that still have plenty of water.

29. **Covid vaccines are still mandated for Federal employees.** Even airlines have fired pilots and flight attendants for not complying with the COVID vaccine mandate. Southwest Airlines have become woke, firing people if they post anything on social media that is against their regulations. They are even monitoring what they say on social media. One flight attendant said, "The Union activists, those who hate the conservatives and the Christians, are actively copying and looking for information that they can use to harm those that they disagree with."

30. **Children mind-controlled:** Schools will continue to force CRT (Critical Race Theory) on children, and transgendism on them. Florida's Governor DeSantis has banned CTR in Florida schools. Your children won't be your children, they will belong to the state. If I had a young child, I would home-school them, and make sure they learn spirituality and compassion for all life on Earth.

31. **The Alien Agenda -** You probably don't believe there is an ET problem on our planet, but the reptilians are a scientifically advanced race (no spirituality) and an ancient one who has been working behind the scenes to control humans. Millions of people have vanished over the decades from their heinous experiments. Our government has worked with them for their technology and allowed this evil on humanity. However, benevolent ETs are working to help us. Also, there are ways to block the reptilian race by using our power thoughts against them. Stay tuned...and watch the skies as UFO sightings increase. UFOs often hide as

clouds indicated in my book, *Lizzie Extraterrestrials Worldwide*. Something huge is going to happen with the alien presence in 2023. More revelations to come from the military.

32. **Watch Florida's Governor Ron DeSantis rise in popularity.** He will be re-elected as Governor on November 8, 2022, and he will announce his run for President in January of 2023. Will it be Trump vs DeSantis?

33. **401 (K) plans hurt by Biden!** Huge losses for those who have 401 (K) plans, but don't sell. Hang on to them! Bitcoin and crypto will continue to fall.

34. **Mid-Term Elections – The Red Wave is coming!** It could be a huge win for Republicans in the 2022 mid-year elections, that if there isn't any voter fraud. There will be a mostly red wave in the mid-term elections, but some Democrats will prevail. Republicans will take back the Senate. In many states, because of mail-in votes, it could take a week and even longer count the ballots. Nancy Pelosi will retire soon.

35. **Children will become seriously ill from the new virus. Some will die.** I find it strange this virus suddenly appeared.

36. **China and Iran and the rest of the world will see massive protests against COVID lockdowns and democracy and it will get bloody.** Humanity was never meant to be locked up in their homes without freedom. Revolutions will spread worldwide.

CHAPTER TWENTY-TWO

Apocalyptic Nightmares

Countless people throughout the world have experienced apocalyptic nightmares after a UFO experience. I did. The nightmares began in 1957 after a disc-shaped object hovered over me and followed me as I walked home from my first-grade school in Twin Falls, Idaho. My recurring nightmares were the same for many nights—I was an adult escaping erupting volcanoes with a group of people, the earth was shaking violently, and then came the tsunamis.

Kevin Day, a retired United States Navy Senior Chief Petty Officer and a former Operations Specialist and Topgun Air Intercept Controller with more than 20 years of experience in Strike Group air defense, including war-time operations. As an expert operator of the highly advanced SPY-1 radar system with years of service onboard AEGIS-equipped Navy ships including the Vincennes, Chosin, and the Princeton. He logged hundreds of air-to-air intercepts of suspect aircraft in both training and war-time operations.

Everything changed on November 14, 2004, during combat training exercises when the Nimitz was contacted by the USS Princeton. Kevin Day was the radar operator who noticed peculiar spot-on radar while flying near Catalina Island. He instructed pilots in the area to change their course and investigate the unidentified radar spot observed by Princeton's radar. The infrared footage of the encounter became known as the "Tic-Tac Incident" and on September 17, 2019, the U.S. Navy finally acknowledged that the three UFO videos are of real unidentified phenomena.

In 2021, Kevin Day was interviewed on the Travel Channel's *UFO Witness* host Ben Hansen. Day described the event on that day and said the white, wingless "Tic Tac" object, approximately 40 feet in length, was traveling at an altitude of 15,000 to 24,000 feet when it dropped to the ocean in 24 seconds. That meant the object was moving at 24,000 mph, an impossibility for any known human aircraft. Day couldn't believe what he was seeing on radar. Our airplanes can handle about 14-Gs before it would begin falling apart and any human in such a vehicle would turn to mush.

After the incident was reported, Navy officers collected everything on the UFO/UAP incident including tapes of conversations between Day and the pilots. Day never heard another word from any of his commanding officers about the UFO, and he sensed the military knew who or what the UFOs are and have kept it quiet for decades. But why? Are they involved with highly advanced beings and is there much more to the coverup?

Then the apocalyptic nightmares began for Kevin Day as he watched earthquakes, wildfires, and tsunamis consume the Earth. He was witnessing the end of days and he knew we all better prepare.

I have witnessed the same apocalyptic nightmares as a seven-year-old after encountering a UFO hovering above me as I walked home from first grade in 1957.

"Ignorance brings chaos, not knowledge." —2014 movie *Lucy*

"We humans are more concerned with having than with being."
—2014 movie *Lucy*

CONCLUSION AND ANALYSIS

The prophecies listed in this book may or may not come true. The future is not waiting to happen on some timeline. We are creating the future with our thoughts, our words, and our actions. The future is malleable and can be changed. It would be as if we were puppets on a string pulled by the gods at their whims. We have free will to mold the future. What I foresee is a probable future on the path we are currently headed. I would think that after

300,000 years of human evolution we would have become more spiritual and caring. Instead, we are angry and hateful, and we have become more out of balance than ever. We are out of balance with the Earth, the animals, and each other. It's as if we want to destroy ourselves any way we can—biological and nuclear weapons, and pollution.

Years ago, I believed that music could heal the world if God sang, and his (her) voice and vibration would fill the Cosmos with love, a love we have never experienced.

Perhaps we worry too much about the future and the fate of the world. Someday we will all die, but why waste time on "what ifs"? The Earth might shift on its axis and wipe away humanity, or an asteroid might hit Earth tomorrow and obliterate the planet. Live each day with joy as if it was your last.

Future probabilities are as common as the grass on the ground and shifting sands. They spring forth from the decisions based on your emotions and thoughts, not some random event. Reality is a mirage. The reality is you create it, but you don't believe it. To empower yourself with knowledge sounds too scary and too much work.

The Cosmos is creativity at work as worlds are created by beings in the infinity of space you have no idea exists. There are multiverses and parallel universes that co-exist beside our world, yet unseen. There is no comparison between their intellect to human intelligence.

Are we the masters of our fate or playing out some cosmic scene from past lives? Like the character, George Bailey in the movie *It's a Wonderful Life,* an angel shows George what his life would have been like if he was never born. His life and actions saved his brother and a whole town from financial ruin. Like George Bailey's experience, I believe our actions affect our friends, family, and even strangers—and future generations. We are all connected in ways we can't imagine.

There is a spiritual war about to take place on Earth, and we will all be tested about our spiritual beliefs. There will be those who refuse to see that the Family of Dark wants to control us in every way. There will be some hard realizations in the future, as well as a few great miracles of intervention from benevolent beings. Even some of the evil humans may retire their roles in an epiphany, a new realization that their part in the secrets of hurting and hiding is no longer required. These times will be pivotal and outrageously filled with the opportunity of many lifetimes. Your greatest challenge at this time is to eradicate fear from the planet. The fear-based vibrations from human chaos and fear have sustained non-physical entities for eons. You must learn to understand that thought is creation instead of falling prey to the mind-management projects involved during the twenty-first century. Intend what you want for the world with your thoughts and prayers.

Most humans aren't open to unconventional ideas and theories. It upsets their religious and coveted beliefs about our world and how life began. It's even harder for most to conceive that advanced beings exist everywhere in the universe and even in dimensional realities beyond our physical world. Perhaps it is our ego that won't allow us to accept highly intelligent creatures that look like dinosaurs, lizards, praying mantis insects, blue people, and ant people. Other ET descriptions include the human-looking Nordics and red-headed beings, but I suspect there are even more beings that evolved in different worlds than Earth and don't resemble us in shape, size, and spiritual beliefs.

In the coming months, your beliefs will be shattered by events in the sky. No longer will our governments and military be able to hide that aliens or advanced beings exist on our planet and even under it.

As one Native American told Dr. Clarke their reptilian anatomy is common throughout the Universe, and all other beings appeared subservient to the reptilian species, or at least they wanted their captors to believe they were. Aliens seem to have a nasty habit of lying to humans. So, what are they hiding from us?

It must stand to reason that any extraterrestrial civilization considering the conquest of Earth, would inevitably have had a technology so advanced to get them here that they would have just taken over Earth or destroyed us long before we invented nuclear weapons. But they haven't, and they show no signs of doing so. Therefore, it seems likely that something other than an interplanetary invasion is going on. But what? On the other hand, if we consider Lizzies terrestrial and have been on Earth for millions of years, why would they kill us? It would be easier to control us and genetically alter us.

There are countless legends of reptilian or lizard beings in ancient texts, hieroglyphs, etching on caves, and oral stories handed down by indigenous people. How can we believe our ancient ancestors were such fictional writers? They wrote down what they observed from their point of view. Many of these ancient civilizations were thousands of miles apart, yet they have similar descriptions of such creatures that were seen as gods because of their advanced technology.

Did an alien race terraform Earth millions of years ago and place species of plants, insects, animals, and even dinosaurs on Earth to see how they would evolve? If Lizzies created humans, why don't we look like them? Scientists say we have a reptilian brain because of our potential for violence and sometimes a mutation takes place where a baby is born with a tail, but there's no proof humans have reptilian blood as conspiracy theorist David Icke has theorized in numerous books. But a genetic creation like the gray/human hybrids makes more sense.

However, there will always be the believers, the non-believers, and the forever skeptics even if an alien was captured and put into a museum or a fleet of UFOs landed on the White House lawn. With our current technology of holograms and how special effects have evolved, how do we tell reality from created reality? Even after the Pentagon released Navy pilots capturing UAPs on radar, flying over Navy ships in the Pacific and Atlantic Oceans, they have no idea what these "Tic Tac" objects might be and how they plunge into the ocean at 500 mph or more without breaking apart or creating a shock wave as well make maneuvers in the sky that defy the laws of physics. The skeptics claim the objects are drones, but there isn't a human drone that can defy gravity as the military has witnessed on the radar. The white "Tic Tacs" have no wings or signs of propulsion, and why would a drone dive into the ocean and continue to depth until it vanishes.?

I suspect that alien UAP activity over US Navy carriers off the coasts of California and in the Atlantic might be concerned that they are equipped with nuclear weapons and that upsets them. The military has denied live bombs on their carriers and jets. In 1945, after the first atomic bomb was detonated in New Mexico, UFO sightings increased two-fold. If they were alien to Earth, why would they be concerned about human activities?

In the last one hundred years, every kind of creature and alien has been witnessed. And there are stories of alien spacecraft that have crashed worldwide and are denied by the military. The rationalization for the extraterrestrial coverup is that we are children and can't handle the explosive truth that otherworldly beings visit Earth or live beneath us or in our deepest oceans. Perhaps that was true at one time, but the public has heard or seen enough videos to know they exist. If H.G. Wells *War of the Worlds* event happened on Earth, no doubt humans would be frightened and panicked but that has not happened…yet. If they were going to take over our world, wouldn't they have done it long before we developed advanced weapons?

Perhaps the coverup goes beyond the fear factor and might involve our military and governments lying to us about our human evolution that we didn't evolve from monkeys but from extraterrestrial genetic labs deep within our planet.

Legends of serpent people can be found on every continent. The Bible, the Quran, and the ancient texts known as the Nag Hammadi codices discovered in Egypt on January 13, 1945, described reptilian entities interacting with humans. In Mexico and Central America, people worshiped the feather serpent god called Kukulkan or Quetzalcoatl. In India, the Nagas were half-human half-reptilian gods who live underground in a place called Patala. And in China and Japan, many emperors claim to be the descendants of dragons. Could these stories represent real Reptilian beings that people all over the world encountered in the ancient past? The Nag Hammadi texts write about inorganic beings called the Archons. Were they the reptile Annunaki found in the Ancient Sumerian records and Gnostic teachings?

There's so much undeniable evidence that the species of reptilians aka Lizzies have bases beneath our planet Earth and in our oceans worldwide, and performed genetic experiments on humans and all life in their laboratories. Those people who have been abducted by these Lizzies have described them as seven to eight feet tall, with muscular legs, having three or four fingers and sometimes claws for hands, and they have a lizard face with yellow eyes and vertical black pupils similar to Earth's lizards.

Earth has many visitors and those who reside within our planet and deep beneath our oceans on huge bases. There are benevolent and malevolent Lizzies who don't have our best interests at heart. As Rabbi Ariel Bar Tzadok stated in *The Secret of Skinwalker Ranch* television series referring to aliens, "Some are good, and some are bad."

Their essence is deception and concealing humans from their true divine potential. They serve their own ends as psycho-spiritual parasites. As one Native American in this book said they steal souls and transform a free-thinking human into a slave.

Portals are available to many extraterrestrials and make it easy for them to travel instantly to places on our planet and throughout the solar system. As the Pleiadians indicated, a world might look devoid of life, but if it is accessed through a portal, there's abundant life. Perhaps scientists should view planets as more than three-dimensional planetary objects.

UK's author and conspiracy theorist David Icke said this, "The reptilian agenda is very simple—they are here hijacking life on Earth, over thousands of years or more to infiltrate human society, to change it into their image, and to centralize power in the hands of those who represent their interests to the point where they dictate from a central point."

Of the stories given to us by Dr. Ardy Sixkiller Clarke from the various Native Americans she's interviewed about their alien experiences, probably the most baffling are the stories of the Blue Men and their benevolence in two wars (Afghanistan and

Vietnam), helping indigenous people and their pets. Do they help other nationalities? We can only hope that more indigenous people and soldiers come forward to tell their stories of the giant Blue Men.

Skinwalker Ranch in Northeastern Utah is a place that defies reality as those who have lived on the Ranch have discovered through the years. From what I've seen from the History Channel's television series, *The Secret of Skinwalker Ranch,* intelligence listens and observes everything going on there and reacts to it accordingly. They seem to hate any digging or probing into the ground or above the triangle area, and that is an indication that this is a portal or vortex opening...but to where? They have no qualms about attacking humans or animals on the property with radiation spikes and balls of lightning.

Can we deduct that the only way to stop the mostly malevolent reptilians is by our faith and prayers when they use mind control and psychological games like they did with abductees Dawn and Steve Hess in Felber's *Mojave Incident* and the story of Tennesy, a Native American, who recited an ancient prayer given to him by his grandfather to stop them from stealing his soul, in Dr. Ardy Sixkiller's book, *Space Age Indians.*

It's time to step out of our bubble that Reptilian beings have been ruling behind the scenes for eons, placing puppets in front of us as their messengers. These puppets often do not understand that they are possessed and taken over by the massive manipulators. Those people doing their bidding are presidents, popes, kings, queens, and others in powerful places. They recognize that they are nothing more than tools for these dark beings who have been controlled through their perversions of lies, sex, and lust for power and money.

It seems the biggest secret the government wants to keep from us is that the reptilian race has lived underground for eons, and they are the wizard behind the Oz curtain controlling our lives in every aspect and creating new species in their labs. But the government can't keep the truth from us forever, and eventually, we will pull back the curtain to find a flesh and blood reptilian at the controls.

What we do know is they have been here a very long time, and I suspect the various species have different agendas for Earth.

Ardy Clarke's stories of the Blue Men by Native Americans are enigmatic to ufology. The only other person to mention blue beings is author Whitley Strieber in his book, *Communion*, but they were small beings and more square-shaped, not giants. These entities appear more angelic than real by the descriptions given by Native Americans either rescued by them or had their lives changed. They appeared more etheric than solid as if they were materializing from another dimension. Why did they help some military soldiers and not others, and was their reason for taking dead soldiers back with them to their planet to resurrect them, wiping their Earthy memories away with the promise of a new life? How would all the families of dead MIA soldiers feel if they knew the truth that their loved ones were taken to another planet? However, Dr. Clarke was told by the Native American soldiers that the fallen soldiers were taken because they had no family to mourn them.

Preston Dennett made this observation in his book, *Onboard UFO Encounters*, that 'despite the extensive nature of their experiences, most witnesses are left with more questions than answers. They don't understand why they've been chosen. They still know little about the ETS, who they are, and where they come from. What their experiences do show, however, are the various alien agendas. We see an interest in reproduction and hybridization. There is a medical agenda that includes strange medical experiments, sometimes healing. The ETs seem to be particularly interested in people who have psychic experiences such as premonitions or out-of-body experiences. Or, as we have seen, they awaken and foster such abilities.'

One last thought—I investigated the still unsolved cattle mutilations in the late 1970s into the early 1980s. I visited one ranch to view a mutilated bull and talked to ranchers, sheriffs, veterinarians, and branding inspectors across the country. Renowned Tom Adams and I were collaborating on our findings.

Tom discovered a large number of cattle were marked with infrared on their backs which enabled the perpetrators to select them at night. It was always the same scenario—the cow or bull was drained of blood but no blood around the dead animals. Certain parts are taken with laser-like precision such as lips, eyes, jaws, genitals, and rectum. Sometimes the animal or animals mutilated were found miles from the ranch in remote areas, and some had broken bones as if they were picked up, moved to another place to be dissected, and then airdropped. In many cases, mysterious unmarked black helicopters appeared after the mutilation. Most witnesses claimed the helicopters made no noise.

Cattle mutilation theories ranged from satanic cults, and aliens to military testing biological weapons on hapless cattle. In over forty years, 10,000 cattle have been mysteriously mutilated across the United States and that doesn't include the international mutilations.

We can only hope more whistleblowers come forward with incontrovertible evidence of UFOs and aliens (a term I use loosely). If Lizzies live underground and under our oceans, they are "terrestrial beings" not extraterrestrial, and they have been here for eons.

I suspect that a big surprise is in store for humanity very soon, and the ancient wars fought on Earth will once again be fought with beings from the sky and under our planet.

2023 totals number 7, a mystic number of the angels. This number is the number of perfection. The number seven is found 735 times in the Bible, there are seven colors in the rainbow, there are seven continents, seven days in a week, seven notes to the diatonic system, and the Bible speaks of seven seals and seven trumpets in Revelation. There are seven sisters in the constellation Pleiades. Nitrogen has the atomic number seven. Seven represents the realm of "divine vibration." It is the enlightened power of the chakra energies. Seven represents spiritual maturity and seven chakras of the human body. Number seven resonates with the vibrations and energies of Collective Consciousness, faith, and spirituality, spiritual awakening, awareness, inner wisdom, psychic abilities, the esoteric, religion, understanding of others, healing, secret, ritual, and peace. Number seven is a prime number like 2, 3, 5, 11, and 13.

In the Bible, God commanded Joshua to go around the walls of Jericho for six days, once every day, and seven times on the seventh day. God commanded the city to be attacked by seven priests blowing trumpets, with the Ark of the Covenant in front of them and all the people behind the Ark of the Covenant. The trumpets and the vibration of the men walking around the walls of Jericho brought it down.

Number seven is that powerful, and in 2023, we can create a new world with the vibration of seven. In the meantime, makes sure you keep your body healthy and at a higher vibrational rate, meditate, and visualize a white light coming into the Earth and encompassing it with the Love vibration.

No matter what happens on our physical plane you are a child of God, and you will live on forever.

Finally word: During the **Red Beaver Full Moon an eclipse falls on Election Day in the United States on November 8, 2022.** A reddish moon will be visible for 85 minutes from North America, parts of South America, Asia, Australia, and New Zealand. This eclipse **signifies change and the collective soul karma and soul destiny of the world.** "The soul karma, or south node, is where we learn our karmic lessons, and the soul destiny, or north node, is where we are becoming." Many lessons need to be learned and the truth revealed.

Sometimes eclipses bring major earthquakes, 7 to 8 magnitude, or major events. Will something happen to prevent voters in some areas from voting? Let's pray that doesn't happen.

Glossary

Antifa - Antifa is a left-wing anti-fascist and anti-racist political movement in the United States.

BLM (Black Lives Matter) - Black Lives Matter is a decentralized political and social movement that seeks to highlight racism, discrimination, and racial inequality experienced by blacks. They rioted, burned, and looted stores in Portland, Oregon in 2021, after the death of George Floyd. The movement has gone worldwide.

Cisgender - denoting or relating to a person whose sense of personal identity and gender corresponds with their birth sex.

Critical Race Theory (CRT) – CRT is an intellectual and social movement. A loosely organized framework of legal analysis based on the premise that race is not a natural, biologically grounded feature of physically distinct subgroups of human beings but a socially constructed (culturally invented) category that is used to oppress and exploit people of color.

Democracy - a system of government by the whole population or all the eligible members of a state, typically through elected representatives. According to Biden, it means socialism by the Republicans.

Draconian - describes **laws or rules that are harsh and repressive**.

In ancient Athens, Draco was a guy who made some seriously strict laws. Rules that are just plain unfair are called Draconian.

Equality - the state of being equal, especially in status, rights, and opportunities.

Equity – the quality of being fair and impartial.

Fascism - Fascism is a far-right, authoritarian, ultranationalist political ideology and movement, characterized by a dictatorial leader, centralized autocracy, militarism, forcible suppression of opposition

Fentanyl - High risk for addiction and dependence. Can cause respiratory distress and death when taken in high doses or when combined with other substances, especially alcohol or other illicit drugs such as heroin or cocaine.

Gaslighting - Gaslighting is a form of psychological manipulation in which the abuser attempts to sow self-doubt and confusion in the victim's mind. Typically, gaslighters are seeking to gain power and control over the other person, by distorting reality and forcing them to question their own judgment and intuition.

Gender Binary - is the classification of gender into two distinct, opposite forms of masculine and feminine, whether by social system, cultural belief, or both simultaneously. Most cultures use a gender binary, having two genders.

GOP - The Republican Party, also referred to as the GOP, is one of the two major contemporary political parties in the United States.

Insurrection - a violent uprising against an authority or government.

Karma - (in Hinduism and Buddhism) is the sum of a person's actions in this and previous states of existence, viewed as deciding their fate in future existences.

Leftist - Left-wing politics describes the range of political ideologies that support and seek to achieve social equality and egalitarianism, often in opposition to social hierarchy.

MAGA - *Make America Great Again"* or *MAGA* is a campaign slogan used in American politics popularized by Donald Trump in his successful 2016 presidential campaign.

Non-Binary - Non-binary or genderqueer is an umbrella term for gender identities that are not solely male or female—identities that are outside the gender binary.

Pansexual - is a term for **people who feel that they cannot be labeled as female or male in gender**. ... The term is meant by the queer community to be inclusive and means "all genders".

Gender Pronouns - specifically **refer to the person you are referring to**. Pronouns are part of someone's gender expression, and people can have multiple sets of pronouns for themselves (such as using he/him/his and they/them/theirs).

QAnon - *QAnon* is an American political conspiracy theory and political movement. It originated in the American far-right political sphere in 2017.

TikTok – TikTok, known in China as Douyin, is a short-form video hosting service owned by the Chinese company ByteDance. It is believed to be mind-controlling the youth of the world.

Transgender - A transgender person is someone whose gender identity or gender expression does not correspond with their sex assigned at birth.

Wade vs Roe - Roe v. Wade, 410 U.S. 113, was a landmark decision of the U.S. Supreme Court in which the Court ruled that the Constitution of the United States conferred the right to have an abortion.

White Supremacy - the belief that white people constitute a superior race and should therefore dominate society, typically to the exclusion or detriment of other racial and ethnic groups, in particular black or Jewish people.

Woke - Woke is an English adjective meaning "alert to racial prejudice and discrimination" that originated in African American Vernacular English.

Bibliography

Clarke, Dr. Ardy Sixkiller, *Space Age Indians*, Anomalist Books, San Antonio, TX, 2019.

Dyer, Dr. Wayne W., and Dee Garnes – *Memories of Heaven,* Hay House Inc.; Reprint edition (February 25, 2020)

Felber, Ron, *The Mojave Incident,* Barricade Books (September 25, 2015).

Fowler, Raymond, *The Watchers II* - Wild Flower Press, Newberg, Oregon, 1995.

Harney, Corbin, *The Way it Is,* Blue Dolphin Publishing, Nevada City, CA, 1995

Howe, Linda Moulton – *An Alien Harvest,* Linda Moulton Howe; Special Limited Edition (January 1, 1989).

McGaa, Ed – *Mother Earth Spirituality,* Harper San Francisco, 1989.

O'Brien, Cathy – *Trance Formation of America,* Reality Marketing, Incorporated, 1995.

Reading, Mario – *Les Propheties, Nostradamus, the Complete Prophecies for the Future,* Watkins Publishing; Reprint edition (May 21, 2015).

Roberts, Jane, *Seth Speaks,* New World Library, Novato, California, 1972.

Strieber, Whitley, *Communion,* Walker & Collier, Incorporated (reprint May 5, 2022) Original book 1987.

Betsey and Oreo
About the Author

The paranormal has always been the normal for renowned Intuitive and Earth Mysteries Investigator Betsey Lewis who inherited her sixth sense from two generations of women in her family. At eight months old, she and her parents had a frightening UFO encounter in Northwestern Idaho while traveling to Southern Idaho. Later, Betsey's parents discovered they were missing two hours during the long trip, possibly from an abduction. At age three, Betsey was communicating with two invisible spirit guides, according to her mother. At age seven, Betsey was followed by a gigantic silver disc in the sky as she walked home from elementary school, and shortly after that UFO encounter, she began to experience prophetic dreams of huge Earth changes. At age eight, she was visited by her grandfather's spirit.

Beginning in the 1970s, Betsey began investigating alien abduction stories, UFOs sightings, cattle mutilations in Idaho, ancient archaeological sites and Native American petroglyphs in Idaho and Nevada.

In 2016, seven months before President Donald Trump was elected, Betsey was shown a vision of Trump taking the

Presidential oath of office wearing a black overcoat and his wife Melania wearing a light-colored coat. Her vision came true like so many of her predictions and visions. Newsmax TV Media featured her Trump prediction with other psychics. Betsey was one of the few psychics to have foreseen Trump would be elected the 45th President of the United States.

Betsey has appeared on numerous talk shows like Coast-to-Coast AM, Ground Zero, KTALK's The Fringe, Hyperspace, Fade to Black, WGSO AM radio in New Orleans, and other popular talk radio shows. Betsey was a keynote speaker at the 2015 UFO Conference in Albuquerque, New Mexico. She has authored fourteen non-fiction books on Amazon and three fictional children's books.

To learn more about Betsey, her published books, her upcoming events, her intuitive readings, and her daily Earth News blog, visit betseylewis.com

Prophecy Now

Made in the USA
Coppell, TX
02 December 2022

87598421R00107